'Abdu'l-Bahá in New York

'Abdu'l-Bahá
in
New York

By Hussein Ahdieh and Hillary Chapman

Copyright 2012, Hussein Ahdieh and Hillary Chapman.

ISBN 978-0-9698024-4-0

This book has been produced with the consent of the original authors or rights holders. Authors or rights holders retain full rights to their works. Requests to reproduce the contents of this work can be directed to the individual authors or rights holders directly or to Juxta Publishing Limited. Reproduction of this book in its current form is governed by the Juxta Publishing Books for the World license outlined below.

This book is released as part of Juxta Publishing's Books for the World program which aims to provide the widest possible access to quality Bahá'í-inspired literature to readers around the world. Use of this book is governed by the Juxta Publishing Books for the World license:

1. This book is available in printed and electronic forms.

2. This book may be freely redistributed in electronic form so long as the following conditions are met:

    a. The contents of the file are not altered
    b. This copyright notice remains intact
    c. No charges are made or monies collected for redistribution

3. The electronic version may be printed or the printed version may be photocopied, and the resulting copies used in non-bound format for non-commercial use for the following purposes:

    a. Personal use
    b. Academic or educational use

When reproduced in this way in printed form for academic or educational use, charges may be made to recover actual reproduction and distribution costs but no additional monies may be collected.

4. This book may be republished regionally or locally without royalty by publishers who enter into a relevant micropublishing agreement with Juxta Publishing Limited. Publishers should contact Juxta Publishing Limited in writing to enquire about the Juxta Publishing micropublishing agreement. Without entering into a micropublishing agreement, this book cannot be republished by other publishers.

Any other reproduction or redistribution in any format is forbidden without the expressed written consent of Juxta Publishing Limited.

Drawing of 'Abdu'l-Bahá by Khalil Gibran

My name is 'Abdu'l-Bahá [literally, Servant of Baha]. My qualification is 'Abdu'l Bahá. My reality is 'Abdu'l-Bahá. My praise is 'Abdu'l-Bahá. Thraldom to the Blessed Perfection [Bahá'u'lláh] is my glorious and refulgent diadem, and servitude to all the human race my perpetual religion… No name, no title, no mention, no commendation have I, nor will ever have, except 'Abdu'l-Bahá. This is my longing. This is my greatest yearning. This is my eternal life. This is my everlasting glory.

Preface

OF ALL the historical, religious and cultural events in the history of the United States, the arrival of 'Abdu'l-Bahá in 1912 was, for his devotees, the most important event of all. Many people—from all parts of society—had the honor of meeting him, hearing his talks, receiving his wisdom and witnessing his benevolence and humility. For many of these individuals, their encounter with 'Abdu'l-Bahá was life-altering: he touched the depths of their souls and awakened them spiritually.

'Abdu'l-Bahá was, according to his devotees, the 'Mystery of God', the expounder and the Center of the Covenant of a new Faith, the Bahá'í Faith, inaugurated by Father, Bahá'u'lláh, who announced that the dawn of a unique chapter in the religious history of the world had broken. "Ye are the fruits of one tree, and the leaves of one branch", announced Bahá'u'lláh to the whole mankind. 'Abdu'l-Bahá came to America to expound on the precepts of the new Faith inaugurated by his Father. He came here to show us by the force of example, the true meaning of being a Bahá'í: humility, steadfastness, equity and kindness toward everybody regardless of his race, creed or place of birth. He showed people how to be a true follower of Bahá'u'lláh.

This book tells of his days in the city of New York. The authors hope that this account will help the reader to:

1. Gain a deeper understanding of the spiritual concepts and social principles of the Bahá'í Faith as explained by 'Abdu'l-Bahá,
2. Understand the social context of the people of New York whom 'Abdu'l-Bahá met and their beliefs and concerns,
3. Learn about the lives of early Bahá'ís, their personal stories, beliefs and aspirations, the struggles and successes they had in building communities, and the development of their understanding of the Faith of Bahá'u'lláh.

The authors hope that this re-telling of 'Abdu'l-Bahá's days in New York City will be both inspiring and illuminating and bring the reader closer to this unique figure in spiritual history whose life will serve as a model of the true spiritual and ethical life for centuries to come.

The authors deeply appreciates the invaluable assistance in preparing this book of many friends including Dr. Tahereh Ahdieh, Dr. Iraj Ayman, Anita Chapman, Bob Harris, Robert Hanevold,

Kathryn Jewett Hogenson, Tatiana Azad Jordan, Rosann Velnich, Dr. Iraj Misaghi, Prof. Michael L. Penn, Dr. Anne Perry, Mike Relph, Pieter Ruiter, Dr. Hooshmand Shehberadaran, Mouhebat Sobhani, Dr. Robert Stockman, Prof. Christopher White.

Hussein Ahdieh, Hillary Chapman

Contents

Preface 9

The Arrival: The Ansonia Hotel 15

First Days: In the Homes of the Disciples 23

Church of the Ascension: Bahá'u'lláh's Message 39

The Bowery Mission: Wealth and Poverty 51

Groundwork for Peace: Lake Mohonk 71

'Abdu'l-Bahá: Teacher, Sage and Pastor 89

"I am the Covenant" 103

The Unity Feast: New Jersey 115

Last Days: Farewell to America 127

Endnotes 145

Bibliography 161

Chapter 1

The Arrival: The Ansonia Hotel

'Abdu'l-Bahá aboard the Cedric

OUT ON the plain of 'Akká in Palestine, Bahá'u'lláh, who claimed to be Presence of God on earth, the Manifestation of God for this Day, ascended a few hours after midnight on May 29, 1892. That same day, His body was buried next to the mansion at Bahjí where He lived His last years.

Nine days later, in front of witnesses and a large group of Bahá'ís, Bahá'u'lláh's Will and Testament, the *Book of the Covenant,* was read aloud for the first time. The *Book of the Covenant* instructed all the believers—to "turn, one and all, unto the Most Great Branch". As everyone knew, this title applied to 'Abdu'l-Bahá, Bahá'u'lláh's beloved son.

For the first time in recorded history, the Manifestation of God had left behind an explicit Will and Testament designating a successor. Bahá'u'lláh had placed in 'Abdu'l-Bahá the unique authority to interpret the Sacred Texts. All Bahá'ís would now turn to him alone as their source of authority.

So it was that 'Abdu'l-Bahá became the living embodiment of the Covenant which Bahá'u'lláh had established with His followers. Guidance and consolation flowed out from him. He sent teachers to carry the Glad Tidings to other parts of the world including the United States. He fed the poor and cared for the sick.

In 1909, the Sultan of the Ottoman Turks, who ruled Palestine, was overthrown. 'Abdu'l-Bahá, who had been a prisoner and an exile almost his entire life, was now free to leave.

When American believers learned the news that 'Abdu'l-Bahá could now travel, they implored him to come to the United States. But they had struggled to be unified among themselves.

'Abdu'l-Bahá wrote back to them:

> ... In view of the differences among the friends and the lack of unity ... how can 'Abdu'l-Bahá hasten to those parts? ... If the friends ... long for the visit of 'Abdu'l-Bahá they must immediately remove from their midst differences of opinion and be engaged in the practice of infinite love and unity ... Under such a condition, how can they arise to guide the people of the world and establish union and harmony between the nations of the earth? ... Verily, verily, I say unto you, were it not for this difference amongst you, the inhabitants of America in all those regions would have, by now, been attracted to the Kingdom of God, and would have constituted themselves your helpers and assisters ... I beg of God to confirm you in union and concord that you may become the cause of the oneness of the kingdom of humanity.[1]

By 1912, the time had come to make the long and arduous journey to the United States despite the physical frailty of 'Abdu'l-Bahá caused by years of harsh living conditions as an exile and a prisoner and of managing a large extended family and a group of followers in exile. On March 25th, 'Abdu'l-Bahá boarded the large steamer, the S.S. Cedric, bound for the West.

On March 30th, after the Cedric passed the Rock of Gibraltar into the open Atlantic, 'Abdu'l-Bahá remarked:

> In past ages crossing the ocean was not as easy as it is now. Up to the present time no one has traveled, with a purpose like ours, from Persia to America. Some have made the journey but it was for their personal gain or for trivial motives. Ours may be said to be the first voyage of Easterners to America. I have strong hopes of divine assistance - that He will open the doors of victory and conquest on all sides. Today, all the nations of the world are vanquished, and victory and glory revolve around the servants of the Blessed Perfection. All aims will come to naught except this mighty aim. Hardship and debasement in this path are, therefore, comfort and honor, and affliction a blessing.[2]

'Abdu'l-Bahá blessed the children on board. Passengers sought him out. Their admiration for him grew with each day; soon, they took their hats off as they passed him on deck. He taught about Bahá'u'lláh and the needs of the day to anyone who would listen. He received telegrams from Bahá'í groups all over the States.

The Cedric crossed the ocean which had calmed down, day by day approaching the continent:

> I am going to America at the invitation of peace congresses, as the fundamental principles of this Cause are universal peace, the oneness of the world of humanity and the equality of the rights of men. As this age is the age of lights and the century of mysteries, this lofty purpose is sure to be universally acknowledged and this Most Mighty Cause is certain to embrace the East and the West.[3]

The huge boat carrying the Master soon came into view:

> We shall be at sea for another day. Steam power is truly a wonderful thing. If there were no such power, how would the vast oceans have been crossed? What wonderful means God has supplied and what confirmations the Blessed Beauty has conferred. Otherwise, how could we be here? What have we in common with these places?[4]

In the evening of April 10th, the large black hull of the S.S. Cedric moved through the dark swells outside of New York Harbor.

The next morning, Irish dockworkers looked out over the water and saw a tug boat pulling the SS Cedric across the harbor. Mist rolled in.

Several reporters had ridden on the tug boat to the quarantine station where they could board the Cedric. Once on board, they sought out 'Abdu'l-Bahá who was on the upper deck. They were astonished at the profound joy in his expression. He greeted the reporters:

> The pages of swiftly appearing newspapers are indeed the mirror of the world … But it behooveth the editors of the newspapers to be sanctified from the prejudice of egotism and desire, and to be adorned with the ornament of equity and justice.[5]

Passing the Statue of Liberty, he held out his arms towards it:

> There is the new world's symbol of liberty and freedom. After being forty years a prisoner I can tell you that freedom is not a matter of place. It is a condition. Unless one accept dire vicissitudes he will not attain. When one is released from the prison of self, that is indeed a release.[6]

Reporters asked him about the purpose of his coming to America:

> Our object is universal peace and the unity of humankind.[7]

> Its realization is through the attraction and support of world public opinion. Today universal peace is the panacea for all human life.[8]

> One of these ills is the people's restlessness and discontent under the yoke of the war expenditures of the world's governments. What the people earn through hard labor is extorted from them by the governments and spent for purposes of war. And every day they increase these expenditures. Thus the burden on men becomes more and more unbearable and the tribulations of the people become more and more severe. This is one of the great ills of the day.[9]

> If all would lay down their arms, they would be freed from all difficulties and every misery would be changed into relief. However, this cannot be brought about except through education and the development of people's thoughts and ideas.[10]

'Abdu'l-Bahá's words touched on their hopes and fears. The reporters took notes as 'Abdu'l-Bahá spoke. They were all keenly aware of the delicate balance of powers between the European states and how easily it could disintegrate into all-out warfare.

The SS Cedric reached the dock. There was a great festive mood at the arrival of the great ship. People shouted greetings from the deck to the dock and back. The crew rushed about calling out instructions and setting up the disembarkation. A deep horn bellowed.

'Abdu'l-Bahá requested that Edward Kinney—whom he had named "Saffa"—come aboard. Edward "Saffa" Kinney and his wife Carrie "Vafa" Kinney, had been to the Holy Land on pilgrimage. 'Abdu'l-Bahá instructed him to tell the other Bahá'ís who waited below to proceed to the Kinney home and await his arrival.[11]

Mr. Kinney went out to give 'Abdu'l-Bahá's instructions to the waiting believers. Mist came over the pier.[12] The Master stepped off the gangplank onto the ground of the United States like a benediction.

Juliet Thompson waited with her two friends Marjorie Morton and Rhoda Nichols, who was holding a long box of lillies.[13] Juliet lived in a brownstone on 10th St. in Greenwich Village which had become a haven for free thinkers and artists such as herself. She painted and wrote and read the manuscripts of her neighbor, Khalil Gibran, the famous Lebanese poet. She was honest and trusting to a fault and completely open to spirit of the age.[14] She had also seen the vision of the future in the Bahá'í teachings and had become profoundly devoted to the figure of 'Abdu'l-Bahá to whom she had already made several pilgrimages.

The three women waited over by the entrance to the pier, pressed against the window. Though others had left following the instructions, Marjorie refused to leave before she had seen him. The car of Mountfort Mills, a local Bahá'í, rolled up to the entrance. 'Abdu'l-Bahá stepped forward to climb into it. As he did so, he turned his head in the direction of Juliet and smiled.[15]

Chapter 2

First Days: In the Homes of the Disciples

'Abdu'l-Bahá with Edward & Carrie Kinney and children

EDWARD KINNEY had been born during the Civil War in New York City. A talented musician, he had studied with the famous Czech composer Anton Dvorák and subsequently worked as a choirmaster, church organist, composer and voice teacher. His wife, Carrie Kinney, had been born into a wealthy New York family. She had dreamed of becoming a doctor to which her parents objected, instead presenting her with a series of socially appropriate suitors whom she all rejected. In 1893, a year after the passing of Bahá'u'lláh, she met Edward and, over the objections of her parents, they married two years later.

One day, Edward's old friend, Howard MacNutt, had invited him to the house to hear "some glorious news". The Kinneys took a horsecab up to the Bronx and that evening learned of the claims of Bahá'u'lláh. As the couple rode home in the dark, it was clear that Edward had been touched by this powerful announcement while Carrie was disturbed by the news though she later became a believer. That night, Edward wrote to 'Abdu'l-Bahá for confirmation. One month later, he received a reply from 'Abdu'l-Bahá written in red ink which read: "You have been chosen".

Since that time, the Kinneys had made two pilgrimages to 'Abdu'l-Bahá and served in Egypt for a year following the Master's request to found a hospital for tuberculosis patients. When they returned to New York City, they opened their spacious home at 780 West End Ave. for Bahá'í gatherings.¹⁶

Now on April 11th, 1912, they prepared their home for a great blessing: a visit from 'Abdu'l-Bahá.

After leaving the pier, 'Abdu'l-Bahá, accompanied by Howard MacNutt and Mountfort Mills, had been driven to the Hotel Ansonia at 73rd and Broadway. His suite was on the seventh floor of the seventeen-floor building and consisted of two bedrooms, a bathroom, and a drawing room.¹⁷ 'Abdu'l-Bahá always insisted on paying the way for himself and his companions and never accepted the financial assistance offered to him by the Bahá'ís.

Among those who visited 'Abdu'l-Bahá that morning at the Ansonia was John Bosch who had traveled day and night by train from California to see the Master. Bosch, who had immigrated from Switzerland in 1879, had been trained as a winemaker and worked for a prosperous winery in Sonoma County. One evening, he saw a friend on the train traveling home from San Francisco. She was reading Myron Phelps's Life and Teachings of Abbas Effendi. The two talked about spiritual matters—Bosch was actively seeking at the time; his friend invited him to meetings at the home of Mrs. Cooper in Oakland. Over the next months, Bosch attended the meetings though he sometimes had difficulty deciding whether to go to his Masonic Lodge—where he had been a longtime member—, the saloons of San Francisco, or the Oakland Bahá'í meetings. He developed a friendship with Thornton Chase which included staying in nearby hotels when they were in San Francisco at the same time; they would talk for a long time about the Faith and John would offer to walk Chase back to his hotel but when they got there, they kept talking about the Faith for such a long time that Chase would offer to walk Bosch back to his hotel. Bosch became a Bahá'í. He wrote to 'Abdu'l-Bahá, "… may my name be entered in the Great Book of this Universal Life… My watch word will be 'Justice.'".[18]

On this cold April day, Bosch rode in the first of three cars rolling towards the Kinney home. 'Abdu'l-Bahá rested his head on Bosch's shoulder and closed his eyes and let himself nap in the sway of the automobile. John tried to stay absolutely still so as not to wake the Master.[19]

At the Kinneys, 'Abdu'l-Bahá was greeted by many joyful faces. He was seated in the middle of the dining room. Juliet Thompson and Marjorie Morten sat on the floor close to him. Rows and circles of people spread out from him with all the doors of the large rooms opening into each other. He turned his head slowly looking with compassion upon person after person.[20]

When he began speaking, a great spiritual power flowed out:

> I am greatly pleased with the city of New York. Its harbor entrance, its piers, buildings and broad avenues are magnificent and beautiful. Truly, it is a wonderful city. As New York has made such progress in material civilization, I hope that it may also advance spiritually in the Kingdom and Covenant of God so that the friends here may become the cause of the illumination of America, that this city may become the city of love and that the fragrances of God may be spread from this place to all parts of the world. I have come for this. I pray that you may be manifestations of the love of Bahá'u'lláh, that each one of you may become like a clear lamp of crystal from which the rays of the bounties of the Blessed Perfection may shine forth to all nations and peoples. This is my highest aspiration.[21]

After the Master had finished, he offered to greet people individually. Many pressed in around him and asked him for prayers of assistance and touched his light colored cloak as he left.[22]

In the back of the crowd, Howard Colby Ives looked eagerly towards 'Abdu'l-Bahá but could not reach him. Ives had been educated as a Unitarian minister and had served in several small parishes in Massachusetts, Connecticut, and New Jersey. He had begun an informal 'brotherhood' of men devoted to the Holy Spirit who met once a week in a Masonic Lodge so as to include a broader range of people than a denominational church. One of the Board members of that group, Clarence Moore, a humble and kindly man, told Ives about his interest "in a world-wide movement which seems to have great spiritual and social significance". Though skeptical, Ives read through the notes Clarence had taken after hearing about this "movement" and was intrigued. He received an invitation a few days later to a Bahá'í meeting and went because of his love for his friend Clarence. Though he went begrudgingly and remembered nothing of it, it was there that he met Mountfort Mills. Mills taught Ives about the Bahá'í Faith over the next few weeks. Ives was much tormented by what he read and heard and, most especially, with the difficulty he had with offering personal prayer.[23] Soon it was the spring of 1912, and he looked to 'Abdu'l-Bahá's visit for answers. Though Ives was not able to meet 'Abdu'l-Bahá that afternoon at the Kinneys, his life was on the verge of being completely changed.

Howard Colby Ives had to get up very early the morning of Friday, April 12th, to make it in to the Hotel Ansonia from his home in New Jersey to try to meet 'Abdu'l-Bahá. By the time he arrived a little before 9 a.m., the waiting room in the Ansonia was already full with those who wished to speak with 'Abdu'l-Bahá.[24]

The reporters there wanted to know who 'Abdu'l-Bahá was—"I am not a prophet; I am a servant of God"—and why had he come to the United States—"I have come to visit the peace societies of America because the fundamental principles of our Cause are universal peace and the promotion of the basic doctrine of the oneness and truth of all divine religions". There were phone calls from believers inquiring about him and letters to be written to Bahá'í assemblies in the country.[25]

Ives was in a very emotional state so he walked away from the others to a window with a view of Broadway wondering what he was

Howard Colby Ives

doing there with no appointment while so many others waited. Then a door opened across the room, and 'Abdu'l-Bahá came out and said farewell to the people with whom he had been speaking. The morning sun gathered all around his cloak, he adjusted his fez which had tilted slightly on his head and looked directly at Ives. 'Abdu'l-Bahá beckoned him. Ives saw no one else near him to whom 'Abdu'l-Bahá could have been gesturing. Amazed, he walked towards the Master who led him into the private room and dismissed everyone else within it, including the interpreter who seemed surprised at this.

'Abdu'l-Bahá walked with Ives over to two chairs near the window. He grasped Ives's hand even more tightly and said softly in English: "You are my very dear son." 'Abdu'l-Bahá looked at him intently. The Master's very being was taking him in. Howard felt as though this was the first time another person had ever truly seen him. The turmoil that had agitated Ives's soul was released in tears of joy. 'Abdu'l-Bahá wiped these tears away while exhorting him to be happy. A long and full silence passed between them. A great peace came over Howard. 'Abdu'l-Bahá rose up, laughed heartily, took him in his arms with a powerful hug and led him to the door. A new life had begun for Howard Colby Ives.

During these days, newspapers covered events such as, "President Taft forms the US Chamber of Commerce"; "the Titanic, largest boat in the world, leaves port for NYC"; "new Packard automobile company in Long Island City"; "NY Highlanders have become the NY Yankees and will start the new season in their new pinstripe uniforms".*

They also printed photos of the Master. The New York Times headline read: "ABDUL BAHA HERE":

> … he and his father, Ben Ullah [Bahá'u'lláh] were exiled by the Turkish Government fifty years ago. "Abdul Baha comes to us on a mission of peace and will deliver one of his principle addresses before the Peace Conference at Lake Mohonk…[26]

The New York City Evening Sun announced: "AN APOSTLE OF PEACE… The keynote of Abdul Baha's philosophy is that men serve God best by serving their kind…"[27]

---

* These are made up headlines based on actual events during the Spring/Summer of 1912.

The New York City Sun had this article:

DISCIPLES HERE HAIL ABDUL BAHA "… [He] was welcomed reverently by more than three hundred of his American disciples yesterday… Catholics, Protestants, Jews and Mohammedans joined in the reception…"[28]

While traditional Protestants, such as Episcopalians and Presbyterians, had made up the powerful families of New York, now the Irish Catholics were in political ascendancy. Jews, while numerous, were still a society apart. They had begun, though, to create aid societies and would soon make a great mark on New York City.

The New York City Evening World emphasized another aspect of 'Abdu'l-Bahá's teaching:

ABDUL BAHA ABBAS, HEAD OF NEWEST RELIGION, BELIEVES IN WOMAN SUFFRAGE AND DIVORCE… members of the sect were known originally as Babists, after The Bab, but they are now called Bahais, after the Bahas, father and son… Of course nobody could be named Baha without having a beard… He has brought a suite of five very Oriental gentlemen… Abdul Baha is really a delightful prophet. He says he isn't a prophet, by the way, but 'only a servant of the servants of God.'[29]

Though New York City teemed with immigrant women who worked constantly in homes and factories for low or no wages, the right to vote would not be given to any women for another eight years.

Howard MacNutt and his wife, Mary, were taught about the Bahá'í Faith from a Syrian doctor, Ibrahim Kheiralla, who was the first person to teach the Faith in the United States. Kheiralla appointed MacNutt as the Bahá'í 'teacher' of New York City. The MacNutts used their home at 731 St. Nicholas Ave. for Bahá'í gatherings as well as the second home they bought at 935 Eastern Parkway in Brooklyn in 1902.[30] They were most likely the first to hold Bahá'í feasts in their home in the United States after returning from their pilgrimage in 1905.[31] Howard soon began to study Persian and Arabic which allowed him to assist 'Alí-Kuli Khán, a young Persian believer who lived in the United States, in translating the *Book of Certitude*, the *Kitáb-i-Íqán*.[32]

Howard spent much of his Bahá'í life serving on administrative bodies. On December 7th, 1900, he was elected to the first Board of Counsel of New York City. He represented the Bahá'ís of New York at the 1909 'Bahá'í Temple Unity Convention', the first Bahá'í

Howard Colby Ives

National Convention of any kind.³³ He also took a great interest in the development of the Baháʼí School at Green Acre, Maine.³⁴

The Baháʼí group of New York City, though, struggled to be unified. The Syrian doctor who had taught many of them had turned against ʻAbduʼl-Bahá and taught his own version of the Baháʼí Faith. Also, two of the main members of the New York group—Howard MacNutt and Arthur P. Dodge—had conflict with one another. Arthur P. Dodge was a popularizer of the Faith who wanted to reach the masses by producing a magazine with spiritual guidance; MacNutt was more of an aristocrat and thinker. The two men had very different understandings of the station of ʻAbduʼl-Bahá. Dodge believed that ʻAbduʼl-Bahá was the returned Christ, a Manifestation of God, but MacNutt thought of ʻAbduʼl-Bahá as a man who had attained his station through his service and spiritual virtues.³⁵

The New York Baháʼís met in privates homes and, as a result, different groups formed around these different home meetings. Each home meeting had a somewhat different understanding of the teachings of the Baháʼí Faith. The Baháʼís in Brooklyn tended to meet on their own. Howard MacNutt founded a Board of Counsel for the Baháʼís there after he was not elected to the New York Board, which met in Manhattan.³⁶ ʻAbduʼl-Bahá, having been informed of the tensions within the New York group, advised it to expand the number of believers serving on the board to twenty seven. Later he told Juliet Thompson that he had done this so that all the different parties, including MacNutt, would be included; he told the New York Board that women should be allowed to serve. ʻAbduʼl-Bahá addressed the Board as the "Spiritual Assembly" so this became its new title.³⁷

Like many Baháʼís of his time, Howard MacNutt had only a partial understanding of the Faith because very few of the Baháʼí Writings had been translated. Pilgrims who had visited ʻAbduʼl-Bahá in the Holy Land had returned with a much deeper understanding of Baháʼí beliefs and practices and were a great source of learning for the Baháʼís in New York City. They had seen how the Master lived his life and had taken notes on his explanations of the teachings. ʻAbduʼl-Baháʼs visit in 1912 helped enormously in educating the believers about Baháʼuʼlláhʼs Teachings. Most Baháʼís blended personal interests and previous beliefs into their knowledge of the teachings of the Faith. For example, Howard MacNutt had been very interested in a form of Hinduism which taught that God was in everything, pantheism, and believed that the unity of religions taught by Baháʼuʼlláh meant the blending of religions. Other

Bahá'ís held onto popular beliefs and practices such as telepathy. When individuals insisted on such beliefs there was real friction between the Bahá'ís.

One thing was certain about Howard MacNutt—after meeting 'Abdu'l-Bahá on pilgrimage in 1905, he believed that the power of love could bind people and communities together. 'Abdu'l-Bahá had told him to tell the Bahá'ís in New York, "My love is my face; take it to them; tell them to see me in their love for each other."[38]

On the afternoon of April 12th, the MacNutts were privileged to open their home in Brooklyn to 'Abdu'l-Bahá and give the opportunity to many guests to experience his love.

At the MacNutt home, 'Abdu'l-Bahá emphasized that unity was the purpose of Divine Revelation—which many Bahá'ís did not realize—and that love was the means of creating this unity. He contrasted this fundamental spiritual teaching with the wars that had broken out in other parts of the world:

> The purpose of the creation of man is the attainment of the supreme virtues of humanity through descent of the heavenly bestowals… It is so, likewise, in the spiritual world. That world is the Kingdom of complete attraction and affinity. It is the Kingdom of the One Divine Spirit, the Kingdom of God. Therefore, the affinity and love manifest in this meeting, the divine susceptibilities witnessed here are not of this world but of the world of the Kingdom… Through His (Christ) death and teachings we have entered into His Kingdom. His essential teaching was the unity of mankind and the attainment of supreme human virtues through love… Can you find in His words any justification for discord and enmity? … If you should announce that Italy was a barbarous nation and not Christian, this would be vehemently denied. But would Christ sanction what they are doing in Tripoli? … Whenever discord prevails instead of unity, wherever hatred and antagonism take the place of love and spiritual fellowship, Antichrist reigns instead of Christ… We have been brought together here by the power of His Word—you from America, I from Persia—all in love and unity of spirit. Was this possible in former centuries? If it is possible now after fifty years of sacrifice and teaching, what shall we expect in the wonderful centuries coming?[39]

Later on that day, 'Abdu'l-Bahá spoke at Miss Phillip's studio on 39 West 67th St.. The large room was lit from above and cast shadows on 'Abdu'l-Bahá's face such that it looked very rugged and even more powerful.[40] To this audience, he again emphasized love and that the expression of love is service to others. He also tried to awaken in the listeners a sense of the importance of the time in which they lived:

Therefore, order your lives in accordance with the first principle of the divine teaching, which is love. Service to humanity is service to God... Do you appreciate the Day in which you live? ... These are the days of seed sowing... This is the springtime of Bahá'u'lláh. The verdure and foliage of spiritual growth are appearing in great abundance in the gardens of human hearts. Know ye the value of these passing days and vanishing nights. Strive to attain a station of absolute love one toward another.[41]

The following morning, Saturday, April 13th, clerics came to visit 'Abdu'l-Bahá in the Ansonia. He pointedly told them that the "ministers of religion" were partly responsible for the spiritual apathy into which people had sunk. Religion must go hand in hand with reason and science or it becomes imitation so they must relate religion to scientific knowledge.[42]

Rev. Bixby, who had written an inaccurate article on the Faith for the North American Review, was one of the ministers who interviewed 'Abdu'l-Bahá that morning. 'Abdu'l-Bahá presented to him a view of religions which showed their common foundation unconfused by theological dogma or cultural variety.

Bixby: "What is understood to be the relation between the manifestation in Baha'o'llah and the manifestations in Moses, Jesus and others?"

'Abdu'l-Bahá: "It is one basis, one foundation. Abraham proclaimed the Truth, Moses raised the standard of Truth. Jesus established the Truth..."

Bixby: "By what authority is BAHA'O'LLAH placed with Abraham, Moses and Jesus?"

'Abdu'l-Bahá: "Today we believe BAHA'O'LLAH to be an educator of humanity, as Abraham, Moses and Jesus were educators... What is the function of a teacher and educator of humanity? By what evidence shall we recognize him? ... For the aim and function of an Educator is to train the children of humanity. This is His greatest power; — that He has power to uplift humanity. Bahá'u'lláh either taught higher lessons or did not. If He did, He has fulfilled His claim..."

Bixby: "Has Bahá'u'lláh done this?"

'Abdu'l-Bahá: "Yes! In Persia especially He has accomplished this miracle of training and education..."

Bixby: "How can we receive more from the Teachings of Baha'o'llah than from the Words of Jesus?"

'Abdu'l-Bahá: "Jesus and the former Prophets laid the foundation of the Cause of God, — the Heavenly Kingdom. But their followers forget and overlook the foundation. Christ said, "Ye must be born again of water and spirit." "As children from the womb, so must ye be born again of Spirit." The essence of His meaning was that His real followers would become free from worldly imperfections; ... These are the real Christians... Now Baha'ullah came and brought a new life into the hearts of mankind... Under the influence of Bahá'u'lláh's words, he (Mírzá Abul Fazl, a prominent Bahá'í) arose to serve this Cause. He was thrown into prison two years; ... Under all conditions of distress and suffering, he was thankful and filled with happiness, ... This is the strongest proof that the Teachings of Bahá'u'lláh have within them the same power to mould and influence human lives as the Teachings of Jesus..."[43]

'Abdu'l-Bahá concluded the interview by placing a large number of white roses into the Reverend's arms as an expression of the "love and fragrance of the Bahá'í Spirit".[44]

Speaking at the home of Mrs. Morten in the afternoon, 'Abdu'l-Bahá approached the themes of the common source of all religions and the continuing and progressive nature of Revelation. This time he described it in organic and naturalistic terms:

> The spiritual world is like unto the phenomenal world. They are the exact counterpart of each other... When we look upon the phenomenal world, we perceive that it is divided into four seasons; ... When the season of spring appears in the arena of existence, the whole world is rejuvenated and finds new life... The appearances of the Manifestations of God are the divine springtime. When Christ appeared in this world, it was like the vernal bounty; the outpouring descended; the effulgences of the Merciful encircled all things; the human world found new life. Even the physical world partook of it. The divine perfections were upraised; souls were trained in the school of heaven so that all grades of human existence received life and light... the season of winter came upon the world; the beauties of spring vanished; the excellences and perfections passed away; the lights and quickening were no longer evident; the phenomenal world and its materialities conquered everything; the spiritualities of life were lost; ... Bahá'u'lláh has come into this world. He has renewed that springtime...[45]

He spoke while standing on the stairs because the audience was so large. At one point in his description of the seasons he said, *"Va tábistán"*, then there was silence. He looked over at his excellent translator, Ahmad, who uncharacteristically could not find the word. 'Abdu'l-Bahá, realizing this, smiled and said: "Summer".

When he was finished, over a hundred people came up to shake his hand, to ask for a blessing, to present their children, or to show him a tablet which he had written to them. Exhausted, 'Abdu'l-Bahá began to make his way upstairs but they pleaded for him to stay a little longer.[46] A taxi driver asked what message he should take back to his friends, and 'Abdu'l-Bahá answered: "Tell them to come into the Kingdom of God. There they will find plenty of land and there are no taxes on it."[47]

Later that evening, the Master was lying down from fatigue. He received a visit from Juliet Thompson and her mother. Earlier that day, 'Abdu'l-Bahá had inquired about her mother, and Juliet answered that her mother was grieving because her son was marrying a woman who did not want to know their family. So 'Abdu'l-Bahá invited Juliet to bring her mother to him. Juliet, knowing her mother's opposition to her involvement in the Faith and, since there was a thunderstorm that day, didn't think her mother would accept but she did. Once in 'Abdu'l-Bahá's room, Juliet's mother approached him shyly and got down on her knees next to his bedside. 'Abdu'l-Bahá welcomed her and comforted her by praising Juliet and exhorting her to trust in God. She expressed her love for 'Abdu'l-Bahá who assured her that his heart knew that. The next day, her mother's bitterness was gone.[48]

CHAPTER 3

CHURCH OF THE ASCENSION:
BAHÁ'U'LLÁH'S MESSAGE

Juliet Thompson

JULIET THOMPSON was in love with Rev. Percy Grant, the rector of the Church of the Ascension, located down the street from her home. This Church was founded in 1827 as an evangelical church and had remained active in social causes. A fire had burned down the original building so a new, much larger, gothic-style church was built to accommodate the growing congregation. Rev. Grant had been appointed its rector in 1893[49] and had come to know Juliet because she was one of the congregants. Their friendship had grown but Juliet was unsure about marrying him.

Rev. Grant had spoken out against the Faith from his pulpit but, after learning that 'Abdu'l-Bahá was coming to the States, he seemed to have a change of heart and wrote to Juliet:

> If his friends in this city would feel any value or assistance in having him speak at the eleven o'clock service in the Church of the Ascension, in place of my sermon, I shall be more than happy to invite him to the Ascension pulpit in my place. I should like to show so important and splendid a person, and those who love him, whatever hospitality and goodwill can be expressed in this town, by such a plan.[50]

'Abdu'l-Bahá arrived in the rectory at ten-thirty Sunday morning, April 14th, and was taken to an upper room as the Sunday school classes were going on downstairs. There, 'Abdu'l-Bahá waited with Edward Getsinger, Juliet Thompson, and the Persian believers who accompanied the Master. Rev. Grant came in to greet 'Abdu'l-Bahá. As the group waited, 'Abdu'l-Bahá teased Juliet lovingly and inquired after the wellbeing of her mother. She, in turn, asked after the health of Rúhá Khánum, 'Abdu'l-Bahá's daughter, to which he answered: "I have put her in the hands of the Blessed Perfection," said our Lord, "and now I don't worry at all."[5]

By the beginning of the service, the Church of the Ascension was filled to capacity. The altar was wreathed with calla lilies. Dr. Grant began the morning with a reading of prophecy from the Old Testament related to this appointed Day of fulfillment. Next he chose the thirteenth chapter of First Corinthians from the apostle Paul:

> If I speak in the tongues of men or of angels, but do not have love, I am only a resounding gong or a clanging cymbal… Love never fails. But where there are prophecies, they will cease; where there are tongues, they will be stilled; where there is knowledge, it will pass away. For we know in part and we prophesy in part, but when completeness comes, what is in part disappears. When I was a child, I talked like a child, I thought like a child, I reasoned like a child. When I became a man, I put the ways of childhood behind me. For

now we see only a reflection as in a mirror; then we shall see face to face. Now I know in part; then I shall know fully, even as I am fully known. And now these three remain: faith, hope and love. But the greatest of these is love.[52]

The choir then burst into "Jesus lives". Dr. Grant stepped into the vestry and walked out hand in hand with 'Abdu'l-Bahá. They stood for a moment by the altar under a mural showing the Resurrection. 'Abdu'l-Bahá was seated in the chair near the altar reserved for a bishop, the representative of Christ who had the church's teaching authority for the City and oversaw all churches in a region. Over the chair hung a Greek-style wreath symbolizing the victory of Christ through His Suffering.[53]

Dr. Grant introduced the Master who then rose and walked over to the steps of the altar. He looked out lovingly over the packed church. As he spoke, he asserted that unity was the purpose of religion and the way to peace in the world:

> Today the world of humanity is in need of international unity and conciliation. To establish these great fundamental principles a propelling power is needed. It is self-evident that the unity of the human world and the Most Great Peace cannot be accomplished through material means. They cannot be established through political power, for the political interests of nations are various and the policies of peoples are divergent and conflicting. They cannot be founded through racial or patriotic power, for these are human powers, selfish and weak. The very nature of racial differences and patriotic prejudices prevents the realization of this unity and agreement. Therefore, it is evidenced that the promotion of the oneness of the kingdom of humanity, which is the essence of the teachings of all the Manifestations of God, is impossible except through the divine power and breaths of the Holy Spirit.[54]

He praised Jesus Christ again, describing the Manifestation of God in terms of being an 'educator':

> Jesus Christ came to teach the people of the world this heavenly civilization and not material civilization. He breathed the breath of the Holy Spirit into the body of the world and established an illumined civilization. Among the principles of divine civilization He came to proclaim is the Most Great Peace of mankind.[55]

He also warned of the spiritual danger lurking in materialism:

> The world of humanity is submerged in a sea of materialism. The rays of the Sun of Reality are seen but dimly and darkly through

Rev. Percy Grznt

opaque glasses. The penetrative power of the divine bounty is not fully manifest.⁵⁶

These ideas may well have resonated with this devout big city audience aware of the very delicate balance of power between the great nations of Europe and mindful in their day to day lives of the many social problems of the poor and needy in their burgeoning city.

'Abdu'l-Bahá ended his talk by raising his palms upward and offering a prayer near the altar, "… Verily, this congregation is seeking Thy path, searching for Thy mystery, …".⁵⁷ Dr. Grant and other clerics bowed their heads as they listened. The service broke up with the recessional hymn "Christ our Lord has risen again".⁵⁸

'Abdu'l-Bahá was taken back into the Rectory. Groups of parishioners moved forward to greet him and seek his blessing. Bahá'ís sang "Allah-u-Abha". One woman cried as she held the hem of 'Abdu'l-Bahá's robe. He calmed her with his loving kindness.⁵⁹

The Master asked to see Dr. Grant, but he had been detained in the Church. Mountfort Mills walked out with 'Abdu'l-Bahá to the car. Dr. Grant's mother then ran into the room looking side to side for the Master. She wanted his blessing. She made her way out to the black car in which 'Abdu'l-Bahá sat. When she got to the car, she knelt in the street. The Master placed his hands on her head.⁶⁰

Juliet Thompson went back in to the empty church to thank Dr. Grant. This had been a day of days for her. For years she had struggled with her attendance at this church and her relationship with Dr. Grant. This had been a day of fulfillment in which 'Abdu'l-Bahá's presence in this church had proclaimed the Resurrection—that this time was the appointed Day. She wanted to thank Dr. Grant who had been so dynamic during the service. The last parishioner had left. She walked up to him. They clasped hands. He smiled and called her, "My darling". Instead of the spiritual energy she had seen during the service, Juliet now saw in his face a strange falseness which snapped her out of her feelings for him. She turned away.⁶¹

୨ଓ ୨ଓ ୨ଓ

That afternoon, 'Abdu'l-Bahá spoke at the Union Meeting of Advanced Thought Centers in the Carnegie Hall building on 57th St. Using the imagery of sun and mirrors, he related the oneness of God to the goal of the oneness of humanity and the need for love to accomplish this.

God's Revelation, like the sun's light and warmth, is for everyone:

> The world of creation, the world of humanity may be likened to the earth itself and the divine power to the sun. This Sun has shone upon all mankind. In the endless variety of its reflections the divine Will is manifested. Consider how all are recipients of the bounty of the same Sun. At most the difference between them is that of degree, for the effulgence is one effulgence, the one light emanating from the Sun. This will express the oneness of the world of humanity.[62]

To receive the Holy Spirit—God's light—individuals must cleanse themselves of this world:

> The most important thing is to polish the mirrors of hearts in order that they may become illumined and receptive of the divine light.[63]

The more human beings do this, the more the world will be unified and illumined:

> This means the oneness of the world of humanity. That is to say, when this human body politic reaches a state of absolute unity, the effulgence of the eternal Sun will make its fullest light and heat manifest.[64]

Love is the quality which God bestows to unify people. Jesus Christ and Bahá'u'lláh caused love to appear in the hearts of their followers:

> All the Prophets have striven to make love manifest in the hearts of men. Jesus Christ sought to create this love in the hearts. He suffered all difficulties and ordeals that perchance the human heart might become the fountain source of love.[65]

> About sixty years ago Bahá'u'lláh appeared upon the eastern horizon. He caused love and unity to become manifest among these antagonistic peoples. He united them with the bond of love; …[66]

Among the many visitors who came to speak with 'Abdu'l-Bahá the next morning, Monday, April 15th, was Mr. Hudson Maxim, an inventor and scientist who was an expert in explosives. Hudson was very interested in issues related to the prevention of international war through the build-up of armaments. In the course of the interview, he attempted to counter and challenge 'Abdu'l-Bahá:

> Maxim: "I understand you are a messenger of peace to this country. What is your opinion about modern war? …"
>
> 'Abdu'l-Bahá: "Everything that prevents war is good."

Maxim: "Evolution has now reached a period in the life of nations where commerce takes the place of warfare. Business is war, cruel, merciless."

'Abdu'l-Bahá: "True! War is not limited to one cause. There are many kinds of war and conflict going on … this is the very civilization of war."

Maxim: "Do you consider the next great major war necessary?"

'Abdu'l-Bahá: "I hope your efforts may be able to prevent it. Why not try peace for a while? If we find war is better, it will not be difficult to fight again; …"

'Abdu'l-Bahá: "In ancient times when nations fought against nation, probably one-thousand would be killed in battle, … but in modern times the science of war has reached such a stage of perfection that in twenty-four hours one-hundred thousand could be sacrificed, …"

Maxim: "Fewer are killed in modern engagements that in battles of ancient times; the range is longer and the action less deadly."

'Abdu'l-Bahá: "… In modern warfare there are bombs which kill men like stripping leaves from a tree…"

Maxim: "The effect of a bomb is not so great as expected. Most of its force is expended upward in the air…"

'Abdu'l-Bahá: "The greatest intelligence of man is being expended in the direction of killing his fellow-man… You are a celebrated inventor and scientific expert whose energies and faculties are employed in the production of means for human destruction… You must expend your energies and intelligence in a contrary direction. You must discover the means of peace; … Then it will be said by the people of the world, this is Mr. Maxim, inventor of the guns of war, … who has put an end to the strife of nations and uprooted the tree of war…"[67]

From the great issues of war and peace, the Master went on to give some paternal and personal advice to Juliet Thompson regarding Dr. Grant. He asked her to convey to him his deep appreciation for his assistance at Sunday's program and that the day would be remembered for centuries to come. He said he loved Dr. Grant but that Juliet must keep her relationship with him, "absolutely formal". 'Abdu'l-Bahá said that the rectorship of the church was in the way of his becoming a believer.[68]

'Abdu'l-Bahá spent the afternoon speaking to guests at the home of Mountfort Mills. Mountfort was an international lawyer who

Mountfort Mills

had become a Baháʾí in 1906 and made two pilgrimages to ʿAbduʾl-Bahá in the Holy Land before 1909. He had begun wat would be a distinguished life of service. He would serve as the first Chairman of the National Spiritual Assembly of the U.S. and Canada, preparing the Declaration of Trust and By-Laws adopted by the National Assembly in 1927, and a trustee of Baháʾí Temple Unity—the body coordinating the building of the Temple. Acting on behalf of Shoghi Effendi, he would appeal the case of the House of Baháʾuʾlláh in Baghdad to the League of Nations, which took him twice to Baghdad where he would have an audience with the King, and be the victim of a brutal physical assault which affected him the rest of his life. The League of Nations rendered a favorable verdict. Shoghi Effendi would write about Mills: "He has truly acquitted himself in this most sacred task with exemplary distinction and proved himself worthy of so noble a mission. I request you to join me in my prayers for him ..."[69]

At the Mills home, ʿAbduʾl-Bahá spoke of man's reality in relation to nature and God. Nature was bound by its own laws:

> The phenomenal world is entirely subject to the rule and control of natural law. These myriad suns, satellites and heavenly bodies throughout endless space are all captives of nature.[70]

Man has a reality which allows him to go beyond nature:

> All live within the bounds of natural law, and nature is the ruler of all except man. Man is not the captive of nature, for although according to natural law he is a being of the earth, yet he guides ships over the ocean, flies through the air in airplanes, descends in submarines; therefore, he has overcome natural law and made it subservient to his wishes.[71]

Man is a part of nature but has spiritual qualities not found in nature:

> If we accept the supposition that man is but a part of nature, we are confronted by an illogical statement, for this is equivalent to claiming that a part may be endowed with qualities which are absent in the whole. For man who is a part of nature has perception, intelligence, memory, conscious reflection and susceptibility, while nature itself is quite bereft of them.[72]

God has given man these capacities:

> The truth is that God has given to man certain powers which are supernatural.[73]

The spiritual faculty connects man to God and generates the love which can bind the hearts of people together:

I am very happy and hopeful ... that the oneness of human world-power, the love of God, may enkindle the hearts, and that international peace may hoist its standards, influencing all other regions and countries from here.[74]

Chapter 4

The Bowery Mission: Wealth and Poverty

Bowery Mission Today

THE FOLLOWING morning, Tuesday, April 16th, 'Abdu'l-Bahá agreed to speak to the homeless men at the Bowery Station on the coming Friday. This opportunity was the result of efforts made by Juliet Thompon.

Juliet had been asked several times by Dr. Hallimond to come to this Mission which served homeless men and speak to the men about the Faith. Her mother had forbidden her from going to that part of town. But Juliet agreed after the third request and used the pretext of going to have dinner with a friend as a way of getting out of her mother's house to go to the Bowery. That night, sleet came down through a bitter cold. The Mission was packed with homeless men trying to get warm. Among the men was John Good who had been in and out of prison his whole life and had just been released from his latest stint at Sing Sing prison. He had been hung by his thumbs in Sing Sing for his violent behavior and had come out filled with hate and believing in nothing. When she spoke, Juliet explained that 'Abdu'l-Bahá had been in prison for years and had come out filled with love. At the end of her talk, Dr. Hallimond requested a visit from 'Abdu'l-Bahá when he came to New York City and invited those men who wished to come to a regular Wednesday night study of 1 Corinthians 13. Thirty men expressed interest, including John Good and his friend, an Irishman named Hannegan who struggled with alcoholism. Juliet later admitted to her mother where she had been, but her mother was so moved by the story that she supported her efforts after that.

So on this Tuesday morning, 'Abdu'l-Bahá gave Juliet Thompson and Edward Getsinger each a thousand franc note and instructed them to change it into quarters and bring these to the Mission when he spoke there. He said that he loved the poor and wished to give them some money.[75]

That afternoon, 'Abdu'l-Bahá spoke with a group of Bahá'ís from New Jersey. He predicted that, in the future, people would think of themselves as having a global, rather than a national, identity:

> The people of the future will not say, "I belong to the nation of England, France or Persia"; for all of them will be citizens of a universal nationality—the one family, the one country, the one world of humanity—and then these wars, hatreds and strifes will pass away.[76]

Bahá'u'lláh's Message had helped to create unity between Persians of different religious backgrounds:

Bahá'u'lláh appeared in a country which was the center of prejudice... They considered the killing of others who did not agree with them in religious belief an act of worship. Bahá'u'lláh established such unity and agreement between these various communities that the greatest love and amity are now witnessed among them.[77]

This unity, this oneness, was the remedy for the world's ills, the grace of Bahá'u'lláh was its cause, and love, its agent:

The body of the human world is sick. Its remedy and healing will be the oneness of the kingdom of humanity... Its illumination and quickening is love... It is my wish and hope that in the bounties and favors of the Blessed Perfection we may find a new life, acquire a new power and attain to a wonderful and supreme source of energy so that the Most Great Peace of divine intention shall be established upon the foundations of the unity of the world of men with God. May the love of God be spread from this city, from this meeting to all the surrounding countries...[78]

He hoped that America would be the country to send this love throughout the world.

'Abdu'l-Bahá, in a moment of rest, again gave Juliet Thompson personal guidance. As he lay back on a pillow with May Maxwell's infant child moving on him, he expressed his love and appreciation for Dr. Grant. Juliet responded that she thought her heart was now "severed" from him but could not be sure of this—only God could change a love so deep. 'Abdu'l-Bahá asked her if she could transfer that love to God, and she assured him she could. Laughing, he said: "That will be enough! I shall try to make no more marriages, when you have *really* given up, he will come after you. I love Dr Grant very, very much, but I want to protect you."

In describing 'Abdu'l-Bahá's visit to the Church of the Ascension, the New York Herald brought up a controversy which reflected the small mindedness of a few churchmen:

Some of the congregation ... and members of other Episcopal churches expressed astonishment that a religious leader not professing Christianity should have been invited to preach and permitted to offer prayer within the chancel at a regular Episcopal service... It was said that Canon Nineteen of the Episcopal Church forbids any one not episcopally ordained from preaching in an Episcopal pulpit without consent of the bishop. There is no provision against a non-ordained person offering prayer within the chancel, it was said, because no such contingency was anticipated.[79]

The biggest story in the newspapers, though, was the unbelievable one about the sinking of the largest ship ever built, the Titanic. Who could have imagined such a thing?

On Wednesday, April 17th, 'Abdu'l-Bahá spoke to people at the Hotel Ansonia about the nature of human knowledge. He asserted that, "All human standards of judgment are faulty, finite". We 'know' through sense perception, reason, traditions, and inspiration, and that all of these ways of knowing are subject to their own limitations. The senses can be easily mistaken such as when one sees a mirage. Reason has produced many conflicting opinions throughout history and the discoveries and theories of one era are disproved or updated in a future time. Traditions are based on human interpretation of Scripture but since the human mind cannot encompass the Divine, this interpretation will always be faulty. Inspiration can be caused by evil as well as good desires. 'Abdu'l-Bahá concluded:

> What then remains? How shall we attain the reality of knowledge? By the breaths and promptings of the Holy Spirit, which is light and knowledge itself. Through it the human mind is quickened and fortified into true conclusions and perfect knowledge.[80]

'Abdu'l-Bahá had invited believers to the Kinneys later that same day for a supper which he would serve personally. He had expressed the hope that both white and black people would come. 'Abdu'l-Bahá wanted to demonstrate the teaching of unity in action through his own loving, service-oriented behavior; he wanted to show that this Teaching of Bahá'u'lláh was a standard by which the devotion of a Bahá'í group could be measured and a goal toward which all Bahá'ís could strive in their interactions with others.

Unity had to become a reality for the world to become illumined by the "Sun of Truth" but this outcome depended on individual efforts:

> The world has become a new world… Therefore, it is requisite that we must develop capacity and divine susceptibility in order that the merciful bounty of the Sun of Truth intended for this age and time in which we are living may reflect from us as light from pure crystals.[81]

The bounties of the Blessed Perfection are infinite. We must endeavor to increase our capacity daily, to strengthen and enlarge our capabilities for receiving them, to become as perfect mirrors. The more polished and clean the mirror, the more effulgent is its reflection of the lights of the Sun of Truth.[82]

Human beings have different capacities but this must not be cause for disunity because diversity was more pleasing than uniformity:

> As difference in degree of capacity exists among human souls, as difference in capability is found, therefore, individualities will differ one from another. But in reality this is a reason for unity and not for discord and enmity. If the flowers of a garden were all of one color, the effect would be monotonous to the eye; but if the colors are variegated, it is most pleasing and wonderful.[83]

On the following day,[84] 'Abdu'l-Bahá gave a presentation on the life of Bahá'u'lláh for the first time in the United States at the Emery home on W. 90th St.; Marshall Emery and his brother were architects, and Henry had designed the front of the Bowery Mission.[85] In his account of Bahá'u'lláh's life, 'Abdu'l-Bahá described a life that would have sounded familiar to those who had read in the Bible about the life of Jesus. 'Abdu'l-Bahá spoke of Bahá'u'lláh's innate knowledge; the boy Jesus, without schooling, had amazed those in the synagogue with his understanding of Jewish Scripture. Bahá'u'lláh had been high born in society but renounced the world to serve the poor; the Gospel of Luke is an account of Jesus's life filled with stories of his renunciation of the material world and concern for the downtrodden. Bahá'u'lláh spent a period of seclusion in the mountains; Jesus was tested spiritually for forty days in the wilderness.

In his overview, 'Abdu'l-Bahá dwelt for awhile on another theme that would have been familiar to Christians: God's Will triumphing over the seemingly superior forces of the world. 'Abdu'l-Bahá spoke of Bahá'u'lláh's Proclamation to the Rulers of the world and of the inexorable rise of His Faith despite His Captivity. He finished by emphasizing that Bahá'u'lláh had born all of that suffering:

> … in order that our hearts might become enkindled and radiant, our spirits be glorified, our faults become virtues, our ignorance be transformed into knowledge; in order that we might attain the real fruits of humanity and acquire heavenly graces; in order that, although pilgrims upon earth, we should travel the road of the heavenly Kingdom, and, although needy and poor, we might receive the treasures of eternal life.[86]

∽ ∽ ∽

Juliet Thompson was born in Washington DC, in 1873, of Irish descent. Early on she showed a talent for painting and was able to make money as a teenager selling her pastel portraits. The money became necessary because her father died when she was twelve, leaving the family with little money. While living in New York City, she had become ill with dyptheria and overheard the doctor telling her mother that she would not survive. In a dream, Juliet saw the face of a "most wonderful-looking man"[87] who reassured her that she would get better. Some years later, while studying at the Sorbonne in Paris, Juliet saw a photograph of 'Abdu'l-Bahá and recognized him as the man from her dream. She became a Bahá'í there in 1901. In Paris, she met many believers such as May Bolles, the first Bahá'í to live in Europe, Lua Getsinger, Thomas Breakwell, the first English believer, and Hippolyte Dreyfus, the first French believer. Juliet had the great fortune to be educated in the Faith by one of its foremost teachers and scholars, Mírzá Abu'l Fadl. She was able to make a pilgrimage to the Holy Land to meet 'Abdu'l-Bahá with her friends the Kinneys in 1909, and a trip to Europe to see the Master again in 1911.[88]

When she moved to New York City, she made her home in Greenwich Village, on W. 10th St., near Fifth Ave. This neighborhood had become a haven for artists and writers, and she fit right in. Washington Square Park, a few blocks south, was the heart of the village and reflected the changing nature of the area. On its north side were the large homes of wealthy business families. These were shuttered during the summer as the families left for their country homes. When they returned and the social season began, one would see well dressed, affluent New Yorkers stepping out of the doors of expensive automobiles opened by men dressed in livery clothes and then onto red velvet carpets protected by canvas canopies raised overhead.

Washington Square bustled with life—much of it contrasting to the lives of these wealthy families. In the evenings, one could listen to a young man preaching fervently about the equality of men and women on the northeast corner of the square. The sounds of a cornet could be heard inviting people to a movie on the corner of Thompson St. and the Square. Children gathered around men who were grinding hand organs. A band of musicians hired by the City would be entertaining people in the Square. A sidewalk cart sold warm chestnuts. Men and women down on their luck slept on some of the benches and were regularly awoken and moved along by the policemen who patrolled the streets from each corner. In the fall, an old white horse pulled a cart around the Square while men dressed in brown uniforms tossed in the piles of leaves. As the weather turned cold, the fountains in the Square were wrapped in straw.

Artists and writers had gradually moved into the dilapidated buildings, cottages and frame houses south of the Square. An artist who was new to the area would have to first make a stop at Pepe's real estate office who knew every room in the area and how to make studio space out of the holes in the wall available in old factory buildings. Pepe would send the newly-arrived, young struggling artist out on the street with a list of places for rent. Every building was constantly in transition from its former uses. One local writer lived in a garret of a one hundred year old building which had begun as a tool house for undertakers, then become the home of a Governor, then a stage-house for stage coaches waiting to carry the mail, then a roadhouse for people, then a saloon and then an inn. Washington Square itself had originally been a potter's field. This area had been home to the pamphleteer Thomas Paine, and writers Edgar Allan Poe, Mark Twain, Robert Louis Stevenson, and O. Henry, among many others. Its cheap rents, bustling atmosphere of small restaurants, shops and tiny obscure theaters—described by one writer as being for, "people who cannot act, who have no originality in any direction, who are amateur playwrights, gather together, rent rooms some where … and play theatre"—were all attractions for artist and writers.[89]

This was an age when more people were searching outside of mainstream churches for alternatives or broader belief systems, possibly sensing that the times were changing. Among these alternatives were spiritualism, the belief that God is transcendent and cannot be described in anthropomorphic terms and that spirits can contact us from the next world, theosophical societies, which taught that God was everywhere, that human nature was ultimately Divine and that sickness could be healed through "right thinking", and Hinduism and Buddhism which were taught or understood only in fragments. These movements tended to have a more universal view of God and salvation than traditional churches, and people were more willing to discard or go beyond long accepted church doctrines. Many of these seekers continued to be Christian in terms of its social and spiritual teachings and some involvement in a church. For some, the Bahá'í Faith appeared to be one of these 'alternatives', with a charismatic rather than formal community structure, and, as far as people knew, with general spiritual teachings such as the unity of the human race and the promotion of world peace which echoed what many people regarded as the needs of the day and which did not challenge their already held opinions on other subjects. In this sense, the pre-World War I 'spirit of the age' reflected some aspects of Bahá'u'lláh's Teachings.

Greenwich Village was also home to free thinkers who had political leanings, most notably, anarchists, who saw governments as oppressive and emphasized personal freedom, and communists, who believed in a classless egalitarian society where government controlled the means of production to ensure social and economic equality. These kinds of political views had grown in response to the terrible conditions of workers in industrialized societies. There were also many trade unionists who advocated for workers' rights. In his talks in the United States, 'Abdu'l-Bahá would bring a broader spiritual perspective to each of these issues by explaining the need for a Divine Educator, the nature of true spirituality, the necessity of both social justice and social order, and the meaning of true equality, among others.

Juliet Thompson chose to live in this powerful mix of new ideas and changing culture when she moved to W. 10th St. This house would also be home to other artists and writers during her many years there. The residents of the house often shared their work with each other. Salons sponsored by a patron where artist writers and thinkers could gather to discuss current topics of interest in art, spirituality and politics took place regularly in this part of the city.[90] Juliet was a painter and a writer and had profound spiritual sensibilities. While she did attend the Church of the Ascension off and on, she trusted her personal experience when it came to matters of faith which helped her to embrace the Bahá'í message. Among Juliet's closest friends was a well-known writer and artist and a fellow seeker: Khalil Gibran.

Gibran lived in 51 W. 10th St. across the street from Juliet. He had been born in northern Lebanon, then a part of the Ottoman Turkish Empire. His mother's family included a bishop in the Syrian Church. Too poor to go to school, he was educated in the Scriptures by local priests. As a young person, Gibran dreamed of creating unity and understanding between the two great faiths which dominated his homeland, Islam and Christianity, and had been in violent conflict a few years before his birth. His mother left Lebanon for the United States after his father was imprisoned for embezzlement. To develop his obvious artistic talents in drawing and painting, he studied in

Beirut, Boston and Paris, under Auguste Rodin. Throughout his life he maintained an intense feeling for the figure of Jesus Christ whom he re-imagined in his writing in different ways than that of traditional churches.

Like many people of this time, Gibran's spiritual beliefs tended towards the theosophical, and he wasn't sure if a Divine Manifestation was necessary but thought, instead, that individuals could perfect themselves and come into contact with God.[91] Juliet visited his studio and praised his work as did Marjorie Morten, a patron of the arts, who was also a Bahá'í. Gibran became such close friends with Juliet that he often let her read his drafts.[92]

Juliet introduced the Bahá'í Faith to Gibran by giving him Bahá'u'lláh's "Hidden Words" in Arabic. Profoundly moved, he described them as "stupendous literature".[93] Gibran also met 'Abdu'l-Bahá through Juliet. The Master's powerful spiritual presence greatly influenced his work, especially his 1928 book, Jesus Son of Man. Gibran's The Prophet, written a few years earlier, would go on to influence generations of people who hungered for spiritual inspiration.[94]

Gibran spent the winter of 1912 as a recluse; he was so absorbed in his work that he would hardly eat, instead drinking strong Turkish coffee and smoking. But as the spring of 1912 bloomed, he began to rejoin the social world. He came to adore 'Abdu'l-Bahá. In explaining why 'Abdu'l-Bahá was such an inspiration for his book on Jesus, he said, "For the first time I saw form noble enough to be a receptacle for the Holy Spirit."[95]

Very early on the morning of April 19th, 'Abdu'l-Bahá sat for a portrait painted by Gibran. They had met three times previously about the portrait; Gibran had also acted on those occasions as an interpreter. The night before he hadn't been able to sleep. After an hour of painting, the twenty-five onlookers in the room began exclaiming that he had captured the soul of the Master in his portrait. 'Abdu'l-Bahá said to him in Arabic: "Those who work with the Spirit work well. You have the power of Alláh in you," and, quoting Muhammad, said: "Prophets and poets see with the light of God". Gibran recorded that in 'Abdu'l-Bahá's smile, "there was the mystery of Syria and Arabia and Persia." In the days and weeks that followed this sitting, Gibran felt a new surge of energy and spirit flowing through him.[96]

ℳ ℳ ℳ

After his portrait was painted, 'Abdu'l-Bahá went to speak at Columbia University's Earl Hall. Columbia University dated back to the mid-1700's and became one of the nation's earliest centers for graduate education. Over the decades, the University distinguished itself for its schools of law, which produced two Supreme Court Justices, its school of journalism, and its school of international relations. It contributed enormously to different fields of science: modern anthropology founder Franz Boaz, modern genetics pioneered by Thomas Hunt Morgan, an integrated approach in medicine developed at Columbia-Presbyterian, and important advances made in psychology.

'Abdu'l-Bahá spent much of his talk explaining that while man was a part of nature, he also transcended it through the use of his intellectual capacity for scientific investigation. Man, therefore, was "the most noble part of creation, the governor of nature".[97] But, as 'Abdu'l-Bahá always did, he now brought in the other dimension of man's life—the spirit:

> As material knowledge is illuminating those within the walls of this great temple of learning, so also may the light of the spirit, the inner and divine light of the real philosophy glorify this institution.[98]

And the main principle of this "Divine philosophy" was the oneness of humanity which was brought about by love, in the same way that the Manifestations of God were all one who proclaimed peace to the world. The purpose of religion was not the negation of reason and science nor the establishment of competing doctrines and sects:

> The divine purpose is that men should live in unity, concord and agreement and should love one another.[99]

'Abdul-Bahá exhorted the students, professors and others to the promotion of religion, "and the religion of God is absolute love and unity".[100]

Back at the Ansonia, one of the many people who had come to meet 'Abdu'l-Bahá was a reporter from the New York Tribune, Mary Williams, who went by the pen name, "Kate Carew". Raised part of her childhood in the mining camps of the California Sierras, she had studied art at the San Francisco School of Design and had become an illustrator for the San Francisco Examiner. After she moved to New York City, Joseph Pulitzer hired her to work at the New York World where she specialized in illustrated interviews.[101] Pulitzer had been engaged in an intense rivalry with William Randolph Hearst, who owned the New

York Journal and whose mother was a follower of 'Abdu'l-Bahá. Pulitzer and Hearst developed a sensationalist form of journalism called "yellow journalism" which sent newspaper sales rocketing; the circulation of the World, for example, increased 4,000%.[102] Several times while in the United States, 'Abdu'l-Bahá admonished journalists to be fair and accurate in their reporting

Over her career she would interview many of the famous people of the age such as actress Sarah Bernhardt, the writers Mark Twain and Jack London, the poet W. B. Yeats, the artist Pablo Picasso, the political leaders Winston Churchill and Theodore Roosevelt, the filmmaker D. W. Griffith, the banker J. P. Morgan, and the inventors the Wright brothers.[103] She approached her work of interviewing and drawing caricatures of famous people with dark humor:

> One broiled live celebrity per week was the diet prescribed and rigorously enforced by my uncompromising editor, and he organized a staff of one, whose duty it was to hunt down the designated victims. The staff would make an appointment, and I would follow with the instruments of torture, consisting of an inquiring eye and a stub of pencil.[104]

… including her boss, Joseph Pulitzer--"Joseph Pulitzer is pre-eminently a publicist in journalism"[105] …

… politicians--"most of the victims were politicians and statesmen--unless it be true, as I am prepared to believe, that a statesman is only a politician who happens to be dead."[106]

… and, of course, lawyers –

> … the history of most of my interviews has been a frantic effort to penetrate beneath the crust of the politician in search of the man. In this process I have discovered many public men to have something almost human about them, and only when they are lawyers do they object to having it known.[107]

Now, she brought her breezy cynicism and caustic eye to her interview with 'Abdu'l-Bahá:

> On my way to the more rarefied atmosphere of the upper floors I found myself hoping that the Baha would tell me I had a lovely soul. They say he finds out the strangest things about you… I felt all sorts of mystic possibilities awaited me the other side of the door… At my finger's pressure on the bell the door flew open with a most unholy speed. No fumes of incense, no tinkling bells, no prostrate figures and whispered benedictions…[108]

After she had waited awhile in the anteroom, 'Abdu'l-Bahá came in. Her cynicism began to ebb in the Master's presence:

> He is scarcely above medium height, but so extraordinary is the dignity of his majestic carriage that he seemed more than the average stature... While slowly making the round of the room his soft, penetrating, faded eyes studied us all, without seeming to do so.[109]

The translator related to Mary how 'Abdu'l-Bahá wept during the play he had just seen, *The Terrible Meek*. She became aware of the power of 'Abdu'l-Bahá's sincerity and heartfelt, unencumbered directness:

> I can imagine repeating his phrases to some of my clever friends, who would be sure to say: "Why, that's as old as the hills. I don't see anything to make a fuss about in that." But the time honored words, even repeated by an interpreter, are so fraught with the Baha's wonderful personality that they seem never to have been uttered before. His meaning is not couched in any esoteric phrases. Again and again he has disclaimed the possession of hidden lore. Again and again he has placed the attainments of the heart and soul above those of the mind.[110]

Then it was her turn to have a private interview, and she was invited into 'Abdu'l-Bahá's chamber. Now, she was able to observe the Master close-up, and she sensed the depth of his wisdom, the result of his close connection to the Kingdom of God:

> His beautiful voice, like a golden echo, follows close the termination of each sentence. The master looks very spirituelle. He is in a relaxed attitude... So much more akin to the spirit world than this does he seem that I find myself often addressing Dr. Fareed personally, referring to him in the third person. "Do you think our luxury degenerate," I ask, "as in this great hotel?" Abdul Baha strokes his long white beard. "Luxury has a limit. Beyond that limit it is not commendable. There is such a thing as moderation. Men must be temperate in all things.[111]

She moved through her questions and soon it was time to go:

> I noticed a trembling of the eyelids and that the gestures of arranging his turban and stroking his beard were more nervously frequent. Dr. Fareed answered to my inquiry, "Shall I go now?" "He has been giving of himself to every one since 7 o'clock this morning. I am a perfect physical wreck, but he is willing to go on indefinitely." Abdul Baha opened the half-closed eyelids to say: "I am going to the poor in the Bowery now. I love them.[112]

'Abdu'l-Bahá and friends made their way down the hall with the Master holding the urbane reporter's hand:

I was invited to accompany them ... Can you picture your Aunt Kate and Abdul Baha going to it, hand in hand, through the Ansonia corridors? Perhaps the guests didn't gurgle and gasp! Perhaps! I did feel rather conspicuous, but I braced myself with the thought of the universal brotherhood and really got along fairly well.[113]

They got into the car of Mountfort Mills, and 'Abdu'l-Bahá reminded Mary about service, truthfulness—and the press:

> Remember, you press people are the servants of the public. You interpret our words and acts to them. With you is a great responsibility. Please remember and please treat us seriously.[114]

The car of Mountfort Mills drove south down the avenues of New York City past Park Ave. and Fifth Ave. mansions of wealthy old American families from the novels of Edith Wharton who summered on their upstate estates, to the teeming tenements of the Bowery on Manhattan's lower east side where hundreds of men awaited 'Abdu'l-Bahá's arrival.

The constant flow of immigrants who arrived by the hundreds of thousands from countries where economic opportunity had been hard to come by and where persecution had been plentiful energized this great port city. Huge boats disgorged Italians, Greeks, Hungarians, Poles, Slovaks Bohemians, Russians, and Russian and Polish Jews, into tenements which had unhealthy living conditions and towards jobs with often even more hazardous working conditions.

The plight of the city's lower classes had been brought to light by Jacob Riis's *How the other half lives,* a book of shocking photographs documenting the lives of the poor. This book woke up the public and set in motion studies, inspections and laws to improve living conditions in the tenements which were home to two thirds of the city's population in 1900.[115] The Tenement House Law of 1901 mandated better sanitary conditions, fire escapes, private toilets and access to light. By 1909, there had been progress in improving conditions and stopping the spread of cholera, typhus, and small pox, all of which were responsible for a very high infant mortality. Still, in 1909, there were 96,000 rooms for rent in the city with no windows.[116]

'Abdu'l-Bahá had commented on the possible ill-effects of living in such crowded conditions:

America will make rapid progress in the future but I am fearful of the effects of these high buildings and such densely populated cities; these are not for the public health.[117]

Tenements were three to seven story buildings whose insides had been subdivided multiple times. What made them tenements was their location in undesirable neighborhoods near the factories, docks, slaughterhouses, and power stations where immigrants worked and by the number of years their immigrant residents had lived in the United States. In other parts of the city, these dwellings were called apartments. The use of the word tenement reflected the economic realities of those who lived in them. It derived from the Latin "ternere"—to hold—to pack in as many people as possible for economic reasons. The word 'apartment' derived from the Latin word 'partare'—to divide—so that individual families could have privacy and greater comfort.

The residents of the tenements worked ceaselessly to build new lives and keep their homes as clean as they could under such crowded conditions. Laundry flapped in the wind across the streets and courtyards. The delicious smell of foods from all over Europe mingled in the halls. In the kitchens people bathed in the sink or portable tubs with water heated on the stove. In larger buildings, a widow had the job of cleaning the halls and sweeping the sidewalk out front in return for having a place to live rent free. Everyone did their best to battle the mice, rats, and roaches that scurried about by the hundreds of thousands in the dark recesses of the building—it hadn't been that long ago that pigs roamed the streets. In the evenings, the streets were alive with tenants preferring to be outside rather than inside their hot rooms.

Another constant bustle in these neighborhoods was that of families moving as much as one to six times a year as they sought to go from 'tenements' to 'apartments' and, if they were fortunate, to New Jersey or Long Island; some less fortunate were going in the other direction—from tenements to less desirable tenements, to rooms, to the street.[118]

The Bowery was a neighborhood which held the promise of immigrant life as well as the reality of its poverty. For two generations, the Bowery had experienced a great rise in crime and homelessness. So, when the Rev. Albert Gleason Ruliffson was looking in 1879 for a mission field where he could carry out the social mission of rescuing the poor in imitation of Christ, he chose the Bowery rather than go to faraway countries.[119]

'Abdu'l-Bahá had spent his whole life in near eastern societies that had no health inspectors, no codes that could be enforced, no governments who responded to the needs of those they governed, no system for improving the common good, no soup kitchens, no homeless shelters, no independent judiciaries. These societies had long allowed the initial civilizing and humanizing influence of Islam to become degraded. If you were poor, sick, homeless, alone, and you lived in 'Akká, Palestine, you were on your own, unless 'Abdu'l-Bahá knew you, in which case, you would be visited and provided succor by his own hand.

Now, on this evening in downtown New York City, 'Abdu'l-Bahá walked towards the Bowery Mission in the same spirit as those who had founded it—to follow God's Will in serving those in need.

'Abdu'l-Bahá approached the Bowery still holding the hand of Mary Williams. Young ladies and members of higher society were there to greet him with gifts of flowers. Several hundred men who made their homes on benches, alleys, church steps, and cardboard boxes went into the Mission chapel next to the eating area.[120]

Juliet Thompson and Edward Kinney met them inside the chapel with large bags of quarters. 'Abdu'l-Bahá was invited to sit on the platform, and the other Bahá'ís sat behind him, including Howard MacNutt, Mountfort Mills, Mr. Grundy, Mr. Hutchinson and the Persian believers. Dr. Hallimond, who had taught classes with Juliet Thompson to the homeless men, asked her—to her dismay—to introduce 'Abdu'l-Bahá.[121]

So it was that the son of the returned Christ stood before these destitute men and introduced himself as a family member:

I consider you my relatives, my companions; ...[122]

He then called them his "comrades", a term that would often be used in the turbulent times of the early 20th century to refer to a fellow revolutionary. The revolution to which 'Abdu'l-Bahá called people was one of the transformation of the human heart through the love of God which would cause a person's heart to perceive the world in a way which went well beyond convention, sophistication, reason, and calculation. All that was weak, was strong, all that was poor, was rich, all that was broken, was whole, all that was scarred, was beautiful, all that was forgotten, was remembered, all that was as nothing was Divine:

You must be thankful to God that you are poor, for Jesus Christ has said, "Blessed are the poor."[123]

Therefore, you must be thankful to God that although in this world you are indigent, yet the treasures of God are within your reach; and although in the material realm you are poor, yet in the Kingdom of God you are precious. Jesus Himself was poor. He did not belong to the rich.[124]

Therefore, you are the disciples of Jesus Christ; you are His comrades, for He outwardly was poor, not rich. Even this earth's happiness does not depend upon wealth.[125]

Our hope is in the mercy of God, and there is no doubt that the divine compassion is bestowed upon the poor. Jesus Christ said so; Bahá'u'lláh said so. While Bahá'u'lláh was in Baghdád, still in possession of great wealth, He left all He had and went alone from the city, living two years among the poor. They were His comrades.[126]

Therefore, we will thank God that we have been so blessed with real riches.[127]

'Abdu'l-Bahá finished by invoking the highest station to which a person could attain:

I ask you to accept 'Abdu'l-Bahá as your servant.[128]

The men filed out into the night. As each man passed the Master, he greeted him and gave him a coin. One of these men was John Good. John said later that 'Abdu'l-Bahá gave more to those who were more destitute. Each man had money to pay for a bed that night.[129]

Mary Williams's "last view of Abdul-Baha was as he stood at the head of the Bowery Mission line, a dozen or more derelicts before him, giving to each a bit of silver and a word of blessing."[130] By the end of the evening she, a caricaturist and interviewer steeped in sophistication had grown, "... a little tired of mere words, dealing in them the way I do, but that demonstration of Abdul Baha's creed did more to convince me of the absolute sincerity of the man than anything else that had happened."[131]

This evening, Hannegan, a local man who struggled with his alcoholism, had gotten drunk again and slept through 'Abdu'l-Bahá's visit which he had very much wanted to attend. He was known in the Bowery as a 'tough'. He heard that 'Abdu'-Bahá would be speaking in Flatbush, Brooklyn, in the coming days. When the day came, he had no money. So he walked from the Bowery all the miles out to Flatbush and heard 'Abdu'l-Bahá. Around midnight later that night, John Good, his friend, found him in his room inebriated. John asked him about 'Abdu'l-Bahá. Hannegan answered, "He is the Light of the World."[132]

The Master was driven back that night up Broadway to the Ansonia, accompanied by Juliet Thompson, Valíyu'lláh Khán and Ahmad. Seeing all the bright lights, he remembered his Father's desire that there should be light.

Juliet exclaimed, "It is marvelous to be driving through all this light by the side of the Light of lights."

The Master answered: "This is nothing. This is only the beginning. We will be together in all the worlds of God. You cannot realize here what that means. You cannot imagine it. You can form no conception here in this elemental world of what it is to be with Me in the Eternal Worlds."

Juliet cried, "Oh, with such a future before me how could my heart cling to any earthly object?"

'Abdu'l-Bahá turned to her suddenly, "Will you do this thing? Will you take your heart from this other and give it wholly to God?"

"Oh, I will try!" She answered.

'Abdu'l-Bahá laughed heartily at this, "First you say you will and then that you will try!"

"That is because I have learned my own weakness. What can I do with my heart?" Juliet responded.

The Master spoke seriously: "I am very much pleased with that answer, Juliet."[133]

At the Ansonia he served dinner to those who had been with him at the Bowery. He spoke of the play The Terrible Meek, about the Crucifixion of Jesus, which he had seen. With great power and in the light of a big round lamp overhead, the Master spoke of the life of Christ, its symbolic inner meanings, His Suffering, and His Crucifixion. When he had finished, no one moved. Juliet had not touched her dinner. 'Abdu'l-Bahá said to her "Eat, Juliet".[134]

After dinner, as 'Abdu'l-Bahá made his way to his suite, a maid walked past who had earlier described the Master as a great saint. There were some coins left over from the Mission trip. 'Abdu'l-Bahá asked the maid to hold out her apron and then poured all of the coins into her apron. After the Master had gone in, Mr. Grundy explained to her where they had all been and of the works of 'Abdu'l-Bahá for the poor. She responded that she would give every cent to charity.

Inside, someone asked the Master if charity was advisable, to which he responded, "Assuredly, give to the poor. If you give them only words, when they put their hands into their pockets after you have gone, they will find themselves none the richer for you!"[135]

As he said this, there was a light tapping on the door. The maid came and approached the Master and said tearfully: "I wanted to say goodbye, Sir," – 'Abdu'l-Bahá was leaving the next day for Washington DC – "and to thank you for all your goodness to me—I never expected such goodess—and to ask You ... to pray for me".[136]

CHAPTER 5

GROUNDWORK FOR PEACE:
LAKE MOHONK

British soldier in trenches, WWI

CHAPTER 5 – GROUNDWORK FOR PEACE: LAKE MOHONK

TWO YEARS after 1912, Europe descended into hell.

World War I caused the deaths of 8,528,831 soldiers, wounded 21,189,154, and resulted in the disappearance of 7,750,919 more.[137] Roughly 6,800,000 civilians died because of famines in Europe, the Ottoman Empire, and Africa, and the Armenian genocide.[138] The War helped set off the Russian civil war which resulted in about two million combat deaths, five million more due to starvation, and an additional two million lives swept away in epidemics.

One in two young men who set foot on the battlefields of World War I perished.

An entire generation of Europeans devoured itself.

People believed this war had such promise. Hundreds of thousands of young men signed up for a chance at glory and to travel to foreign lands. It was going to be a "Great", and short, war. Once it began, though, Europe spiraled out of control with each means of killing having to be topped by an even more destructive means.

At the second Battle of Ypres on April 22, 1915, the French soldiers who were holding the line could see a yellow-green gas cloud rolling towards them. They thought it was a trick with the Germans behind the cloud. They thought the cloud was a trick hiding the Germans, so they held the line. The cloud of chlorine gas engulfed them and when the soldiers breathed in, the chlorine entered their airwaves and burned their respiratory systems.[139]

So the other side responded by developing its own use of chlorine gas. But with chlorine, the coughing it caused did not allow the gas to enter the soldier's lungs quickly enough so Phosgene was used which did not make the soldier cough, and, therefore, he inhaled more and died sooner. Then mustard gas came into use which caused severe internal and external blistering.[140]

The Great War started off fast. But hundreds of miles of deep trenches were built with a 'no man's land' between them, and the Great War became an endless, violent slog. 'Life' in the trenches meant … rainwater turning the ground into mud which caused 'trench foot'— gangrene brought on by the soldiers' permanently wet feet, followed by the amputation of their legs … millions of brown rats running across the men's faces at night, gnawing at the corpses … the never ending lice causing 'trench fever' which could only be cured by leaving the trench for twelve weeks … relieving the 'stand to' at dawn with the 'morning hate' when the soldiers discharged intense machine gunfire at the opponent on the other side of no man's land ... the novice, who can't control his curiosity, raising his head above the trench to look around and then is shot by a sniper [141]...

Shells fell constantly, giving soldiers in the trenches 'shell shock'—a term used to describe extreme trauma resulting in corresponding physiological reactions: snipers losing their site, soldiers who had used bayonets in others faces developing severe facial tics, those who had knifed the enemy soldier in the abdomen developing extreme stomach cramps, uncontrollable diarrhea, constant, extreme anxiety ... many symptoms only beginning after the war had ended.[142]

The hidden costs of war included broken lives, constant nightmares, abandoned families, inability to sleep and eat regularly, to be 'normal'. Studies began to proliferate about what caused shell shock. What had happened to these men—was it their nerves, their psyches? Were they abnormal? Could a man who had plunged a bayonet into his fellow man and seeing the expression on his face and in his eyes really return to normal life?

Wilfred Owen entered World War I as a shy, sensitive and deeply religious English boy, who sought to understand God's Will and live life in imitation of Christ. He set his memories of the War down in poems. He was remembering being in the trenches, shells dropping constantly, when he wrote "The Sentry", a poem about coming across an injured sentry in a trench:

There we herded from the blast
Of whizz-bangs, but one found our door at last, Buffeting eyes and breath, snuffing the candles,
And thud! flump! thud! down the steep steps came thumping
And splashing in the flood, deluging muck -
The sentry's body; then his rifle, handles
Of old Boche bombs, and mud in ruck on ruck.
We dredged him up, for killed, until he whined
"O sir, my eyes - I'm blind, - I'm blind, I'm blind!"
Coaxing, I held a flame against his lids
And said if he could see the least blurred light
He was not blind; in time he'd get all right.
"I can't," he sobbed. Eyeballs, huge-bulged like squids
Watch my dreams still; but I forgot him there
In posting Next for duty, and sending a scout
To beg a stretcher somewhere, and floundering about
To other posts under the shrieking air.[143]

Combat shell shocked Wilfred Owens. He was taken to a hospital to recover and then returned to the front. Back in combat, he was no longer the sensitive boy with a heart that aspired but a hardened soldier who had let go of Jesus in no man's land. In Shrewsbury, England, on November 11th, 1918, the doorbell rang at the Owens home; a telegram arrived informing his parents that their son Wilfred had been killed. On November 4th, one week before the end of the war, German machine gun fire found him. He was twenty-five years old.[144]

So when 'Abdu'l-Bahá returned to New York City from Washington DC and spoke about peace, he wasn't the grandfather speaking in reassuring tones to his little granddaughter, the teacher admonishing children in the playground about getting along, the benevolent patriarch offering the vague promise of salvation. He spoke on behalf of every young man who would breathe in mustard gas which turned his insides and outsides into blisters, who would die in a trench and whose body would be gnawed by rats, who was terrified at the moment of being attacked and, clutching his rosary, could turn nowhere for help … He spoke for the woman who would wake up frightened in the night wondering why her husband kept jumping up and screaming, failing at everything, leaving their children, wandering the streets, disappearing … who lived out her years as an embittered lonely widow taking tickets on the streets of Paris so a person could use the public lavatory …

Or, as the Master put it:

> What shall atone for the sufferings and grief of mothers who have so tenderly cared for their sons? What sleepless nights they have spent, and what days of devotion and love they have given to bring their children to maturity! Yet the savagery of these warring rulers causes great numbers of their victims to be torn and mutilated in a day. What ignorance and degradation, yea even greater than the ferocious beasts themselves![145]

In the days after his return from Washington DC, 'Abdu'l-Bahá focused on peace as the most urgent issue facing the world.

In these talks, he gave people a broader worldview than the ones to which they had been accustomed and a framework in which all could work harmoniously towards peace. The cornerstone of this worldview was that God is one and reality is one. The more people investigate reality and free themselves from man-made traditions, the greater will be the unity between them, and war will give way to peace. The Manifestations of God had all taught reality and these Teachings were the source of unity and progress.

At the Unity Church in Montclair, New Jersey, on May 12th, the Master spoke on the oneness of God and His Revelations:

> ... the human is finite while the essence of Divinity is infinite. Whatever comes within the sphere of human comprehension must be limited and finite. As the essence of Divinity transcends the comprehension of man, therefore God brings forth certain Manifestations of the divine Reality upon Whom He bestows heavenly effulgences in order that They may be intermediaries between humanity and Himself. These holy Manifestations or Prophets of God are as mirrors which have acquired illumination from the Sun of Truth, ...[146]

> The Sun of Divinity and of Reality has revealed itself in various mirrors. Though these mirrors are many, yet the Sun is one... Consider how one and the same light has reflected itself in the different mirrors or manifestations of it. There are certain souls who are lovers of the Sun; they perceive the effulgence of the Sun from every mirror ... those who adore the mirror and are attached to it become deprived of witnessing the light of the Sun when it shines forth from another mirror.[147]

> As this is the radiant century, it is my hope that the Sun of Truth may illumine all humanity... may souls become resuscitated and consort together in the utmost harmony as recipients of the same light... May the light of love shine forth and illumine hearts, and may human lives be cemented and connected until all of us may find agreement and tranquility beneath the same tabernacle and with the standard of the Most Great Peace above us move steadily onward.[148]

In the guest book of the church, he wrote this prayer:

> ... Even in this Church we have raised our voice to Thy Kingdom like unto Elijah. O God! Attract the members of this Church to thy Beauty, ...[149]

Later that day, the Master spoke at a meeting of the International Peace Forum, held in the Grace Methodist Episcopal on W. 104th St.. The International Peace Forum would go on to publish speeches on peace by President William Howard Taft (1909-1913). President Taft—later named the Chief Justice of the United States Supreme Court—believed that world peace could most effectively be brought about through international arbitration.[150] After the cataclysm of World War I, he pushed for a strong League of Nations to prevent war.

When 'Abdu'l-Bahá spoke at the International Peace Forum, he emphasized that religion was one because it dealt with reality but people had created imaginary distinctions which then led to conflict:

Inasmuch as all are founded upon one reality which is love and unity, the wars and dissensions which have characterized the history of religion have been due to imitations and superstitions which arise afterward...[151]

Other wars are caused by purely imaginary racial differences; for humanity is one kind, one race and progeny, inhabiting the same globe. In the creative plan there is no racial distinction and separation ... Therefore, false distinctions of race and native land, which are factors and causes of warfare, must be abandoned...[152]

Religions were "founded upon one reality which is love and unity", and existed for peace. Bahá'u'lláh had come to bring about "the Most Great Peace and international arbitration". He ...

...wrote to all the kings and rulers, encouraging, advising and admonishing them in regard to the establishment of peace, making it evident by conclusive proofs that the happiness and glory of humanity can only be assured through disarmament and arbitration.

It was the Divine Intention that human beings love one another and that the Divine Intention surely must be superior to that of the human being:

If God did not love all, He would not have created, trained and provided for all. Loving-kindness is the divine policy. Shall we consider human policy and attitude superior to the wisdom and policy of God?[153]

The following day, May 13th, at his talk before the New York Peace Society in the Astor Hotel, 'Abdu'l-Bahá elaborated on these points:

From the prison of 'Akká He (Bahá'u'lláh) addressed the kings and rulers of the earth in lengthy letters, summoning them to international agreement and explicitly stating that the standard of the Most Great Peace would surely be upraised in the world... This has come to pass. The powers of earth cannot withstand the privileges and bestowals which God has ordained for this great and glorious century... Man can withstand anything except that which is divinely intended and indicated for the age and its requirements...[154]

The age which Bahá'u'lláh's life had ushered in would be characterized by peace and unity and no human power could stop this. The Master praised the 'human power' of the peacemakers as Jesus had done in the Beatitudes:

Now—praise be to God!—in all countries of the world, lovers of peace are to be found, and these principles are being spread among mankind, especially in this country...[155]

The individuals who introduced 'Abdu'l-Bahá at the New York Peace Society Meeting all reflected an ecumenical spirit and willingness on the part of the peacemakers of that time to work together. Each echoed ideas which 'Abdu'l-Bahá had set forth in his talks. The Rabbi Dr. Wise hoped that they—people of different faiths—were "meeting not at all in the spirit of tolerance and toleration, but in the spirit of fellowship"[156] and that "religion and war are incompatible terms".[157] Mrs. Anna Spencer, a member of the Ethical Society, an organization which stressed human potential, individual responsibility, and dialogue for the betterment of the world, noted that the causes of war were racial and religious prejudice and the desire of one group for domination over another. Dr. Percy Grant of the Church of the Ascension, said "we must get down below our discussion of Christian, Hebrew, Ethical Culture, whatever the discussion may be, to the spirit of life and of brotherhood".[158] Prof. William Jackson from Columbia University, who had been to the site of the Báb's execution in Tabríz, asserted that "he (the Báb) was a martyr to Peace and Love"[159] and that "his Successor ('Abdu'l-Bahá) comes to us from the Orient to assure us that this Message of Peace is still being sounded and that we in the West and they in the East are really one in heart".[160]

The New York Peace Society had itself been one of the groups of "lovers of peace". It was the oldest Peace Society in the United States having been in existence in several incarnations since 1815, and, in the years before World War I, had gotten the backing of the very wealthy industrialist, Andrew Carnegie.[161] While essentially pacifist in nature, it was not passive—it pushed for courts of arbitration within which nations could resolve their disputes, supported President Taft's view that international arbitration was the path to international peace and called for the establishment of a "Supreme Court for International Justice"[162] through a Congressional resolution. While non-denominational in affiliation, its mission was couched in terms of 'true religion' and the 'spirit of Christianity'. Its parent group, the American Peace Society, launched a petition which resulted in the Hague Convention of 1907, an international meeting convened to draw up guidelines and resolutions for an internal structure for arbitration between nations.

On May 14th, 'Abdu'l-Bahá left New York City to participate in the most important public event he would attend in the United States: the Peace Conference at Lake Mohonk, organized by the International

Peace Society. He took the train up to the town of New Paltz, New York, where he and his entourage were picked up by landaus sent by the Conference organizers.[163] 'Abdu'l-Bahá was overjoyed as they rolled through the mountainous countryside:

> ...he was so exhilarated by the beauty of nature, charming sceneries of mountains, valleys, plains and the verdant forest of trees and wild flowers that he ['Abdu'l-Bahá] burst into songs of happiness commanding others also to sing. Lua and Fareed sang some Persian songs written by Abdul Baha, then Mr. Mills being a good singer was asked to sing. All through the seven miles [sic] drive the party of four sung in whole and in turn while Abdul Baha out of the sheer joy applauded them. It was a never [sic] memorable incident which has seldom happened in the life of the Master and Doctor Fareed could not remember throughout all his service and travel with Abdul Baha of a similar occasion.[164]

The property on Lake Mohonk where the Conference was being held had been purchased by Albert and Alfred Smiley in 1869[165] with the money that Albert and his wife had saved. Alfred, who had run a farm in upstate New York, helped him develop it. The brothers worked on the property with an eye for conservation and beauty. They kept much of the wilderness and also added gardens and hiking paths dotted with gazebos where visitors could take in the views.[166] The hotel built by the lake consisted of nine buildings of eclectic architecture from castles to chalets which were surrounded by rolling hills, forest and gardens.[167] Their intention was to develop a spiritual retreat which could serve as a place to cultivate progressive ideas for the betterment of the world.

The impetus for organizing the Peace Conferences came from the Quakerism of the Smiley brothers. Quakerism was a form of Christianity that had its roots in mid-17th century England. It taught the possibility of an authentic personal relationship with God and the importance of living a life which testified to the truth of that relationship. While Quakers did not have a specific creed, they were intensely Christian in their devotion to Scripture.[168] To testify to the presence of God within them, the "Inner Light", Quakers worked for the abolition of slavery—excluding anyone from membership after 1776 who did not free their slaves—,[169] the advancement of the rights of women, prison reform,[170] better treatment of patients in asylums, the rights of Indians, and the alleviation of poverty, and they worked against war of all kinds.[171]

The International Peace Society, also known as the Society for the Promotion of Universal and Permanent Peace or the London Peace Society, was founded in 1816 by Albert K. Smiley who was a

Lake Mohonk Conference Center today

philanthropist, had served as the Secretary of the Interior of the United States, and had run a Friends School.[172] The Society organized the Lake Mohonk Conferences on International Arbitration which had been held every year since 1895 to gather like-minded people together and "for the purpose of creating and directing public sentiment in favor of international arbitration, arbitration treaties and an international court".[173] It had brought hundreds of important leaders from different walks of life including William Howard Taft and Andrew Carnegie, who founded the Carnegie Endowment for Peace through his contact with the Smiley brothers. This Conference had played an important role in bringing about major peace efforts such as the Hague Conference, the World Peace Foundation and the League to Enforce Peace.[174]

Prior to this visit by 'Abdu'l-Bahá, several Bahá'ís had been in regular contact with the Smiley brothers and the organizers of the Lake Mohonk Conference. Mason Remey had written to Albert Smiley on April 25th, 1911, and introduced the Bahá'í Faith to him as a "peace movement along religious lines".[175] He included with the letter an essay on the Faith entitled "The Esperanto of Religions" in which he boldly asserted that, "Its (the Bahá'í Faith) unique object and mission is establishing a universal religion embracing all peoples, religions and races, thus forming the spiritual basis of the great universal civilization which is so rapidly approaching".[176] Mírzá 'Alí Kuli Khán who lived in Washington DC because of his job as the Charge d'Affaires at the Persian Embassy and who helped with much of the correspondence between 'Abdu'l-Bahá and the Bahá'ís in the United States, was invited to speak at the 1911 conference as a part of the international section of the program. He did not mention the Bahá'í Faith but his talk echoed the statements of 'Abdu'l-Bahá. He praised the American nation for promoting "international comity"[177] and "human solidarity",[178] encouraged the peace movement to educate the people of the world in such principles, advocated for a greater concern for poorer nations by richer nations, and defended the potential of Persia by enumerating many of the progressive steps which were being made in Persia at that time and asserting that Persia had a vey distinguished history.[179]

The main contact for the invitation of 'Abdu'l-Bahá to the Lake Mohonk Conference was Mírzá Ahmad Sohráb. Sohráb, a Bahá'í living in Washington DC, was the treasurer of the Persian American Educational Society, an organization founded to "bring these two countries together in ties of mutual interests: commercial, educational, moral and intellectual".[180] On September 1st, 1911, he forwarded two tablets by 'Abdu'l-Bahá for Mr. Smiley, dated August 22nd, 1911, which Sohráb had translated. In the cover letter, Sohráb states that, "having written to Him ('Abdu'l-Bahá) about the Lake Mohonk Conference and its objects and the courtesy you extended to me, he writes you these wonderful "Tablets"."[181] 'Abdu'l-Bahá in these tablets expressed his great respect for the efforts the Conference had made in the cause of peace, and how Bahá'u'lláh had established the principle of the oneness of humanity in this century and the need for universal peace.[182]

Around this same time, 'Alí-Kuli Khán had received from Mr. Phillips, the secretary of the Lake Mohonk Conference, the compilation of talks—which included his—from the previous year's Conference, and Khán wrote back that he would forward this book of talks on peace to the Persian government and to some of the "leaders of public opinion"[183] in Persia.[184]

Sohráb acted as the coordinator between 'Abdu'l-Bahá and the Conference organizers;* he distributed autographed photographs of the Master and prepared a statement on his visit under the heading of the Persian American Educational Society. This statement described 'Abdu'l-Bahá as the "head and center of the Bahai Movement", Bahá'u'lláh as an "Advocate for Peace", and the Bahá'í Faith as a movement for religious unity and world peace with followers in the "millions".[185] 'Abdu'l-Bahá cabled Mr. Phillips on May 4th that he would speak on, "The oneness of the reality of human kind".[186]

'Alí-Kuli Khán wrote Mr. Phillips that he would not be able to attend the conference due to his embassy duties.[187] A circular went out from Mr. Phillips to the newspapers announcing the Conference and described it in terms of creating interest and curiosity in the "approaching Third Hague Conference, the proposed international court of arbitral justice, and arbitration treaties, general and particular." One of the major goals of these Hague Conferences was to create an international court of arbitration within which nations would resolve their disputes instead of resorting to warfare; as the circular went

---

*   In November, 2011, Sohráb wrote to Mr. Phillips that 'Abdu'l-Bahá was in London and that he was going to meet him in Paris as a part of his work with the Persian American Educational Society. 'Abdu'l-Bahá would be visiting the United States, and Sohráb offered that he might be able to persuade 'Abdu'l-Bahá to come to the Lake Mohonk Peace Conference if Mr. Smiley invited 'Abdu'l-Bahá directly. A reply came quickly from Mr. Phillips expressing interest in having 'Abdu'l-Bahá come to the 1912 Conference. Sohráb wrote back from Paris to Mr. Phillips that he would be returning to the United States in January with a letter of acceptance and an autographed photograph from 'Abdu'l-Bahá. (Swarthmore College Peace Collection)

Lua Getsinger & Sohrab

around, an arbitration treaty was being written between France and England which was supported by President Taft.[188]

'Abdu'l-Bahá's presentation took place in the evening of Wednesday, May 15th, as a part of the international section of the Conference.[189] Some two-hundred and fifty guests were present for the address.[190] The Master extolled the new century:

> This is the century of light and of bounty. In the past, the unity of patriotism, the unity of nations and religions was established; hence this century is greater than the past.[191]

The Master then introduced the figure of Bahá'u'lláh:

> At such a time as this (a time of turmoil and war), His Holiness, Baha'u'llah appeared. He proclaimed the oneness of the world of humanity and the greatest peace (Most Great Peace). He wrote to all the kings and addressed epistles to all the religionists of Persia, and all the souls who accepted His platform and emulated and followed His teachings—whether Christians, Mohammedans, Jews or Zoroastrians—were united and attained the greatest amity and unity.[192]

'Abdu'l-Bahá followed this universal declaration of a new day by listing eight principles of Bahá'u'lláh, including the investigation of reality for oneself, the oneness of humanity, the equality of men and women, the agreement of science and true religion, the eradication of all forms of prejudice, the appearance of social justice through the moderation of wealth and poverty, religion and the necessity of the Holy Spirit in changing human society.[193] In fifteen minutes or less, the Master had made the Great Announcement directly and fully to this distinguished audience of people who were working towards the common goal of world peace.

Sohráb sent a telegram later at night to Agnes Parsons, a Bahá'í in Washington DC, that 'Abdu'l-Bahá's presence and words had "fired the hearts"[194] of the attendees because the talk had been like a "conflagration"[195] which was met with the longest applause of the evening. The audience would have wanted the Master to speak longer but he was fatigued. Many sought to shake his hand, and Mr. Smiley praised 'Abdu'l-Bahá and spoke reverently about the new teachings. Mrs. Smiley presented 'Abdu'l-Bahá with a pendant from the conference.[196] Later on that summer, a prominent Reverend from New York would remember the talk as the "most remarkable"[197] one he had ever heard.

The Master received the kind words with graciousness and equanimity. But what he wanted was action. To Dr. Zia Baghdadi, who was with him at Mohonk, he said:

> Once I wrote to the friends in Persia with regard to peace congresses and conferences, that if the members of the conferences do not succeed in practicing what they say, they may be compared to those who hold a meeting to discuss and form firm resolutions about the sinfulness and harmfulness of liquors, but, after having the meeting, occupy themselves in selling liquors… Now we must not only think and talk peace but we must develop the power to practice peace so that… peace may permeate the whole world.[198]

The Master stayed at the scenic resort for another day. Photographs of him were taken, he blessed many with kind words, smiles, and solicitous advice. He told Dr. Bahgdadi that he wished he had a Persian rug to give Mr. Smiley as a gift. Dr. Baghdadi rushed back to the City by train that very night, picked up the rug at their apartment in the pre-dawn hours, made it back to the Mohonk area by train and arrived at the Conference center—after hitching a ride on the mailman's wagon—just as the Master was shaking Mr. Smiley's hand. And then the Master departed for New York City.

The Lake Mohonk Conference came and went but the Third Hague Conference never took place as the violent eruption of World War I could not be stopped by human agency.

While the Hague Conferences did not succeed in their goals, they prefigured the international institutions which would develop later in the century, and the development of a body of international law which would allow nations to come to agreement in a wide variety of areas, from peace-keeping to the environment, from world trade to the oceans and outer space, from economic development to the rights of children.

And while the Lake Mohonk Peace Conferences didn't stop the catastrophe of World War I the determined efforts by the peacemakers of the world did change history.

- In the first decade of the 20th century there were wars of many kinds. In the last decade of the 20th century most wars would be intra-state wars—civil wars, and non-state conflict (terrorism), not inter-state conflicts of which there are about four in 2012 (US/Afghanistan, N. Korea/S. Korea (a 'cold' conflict), India/Pakistan, and Congo/neighboring states)
- In gross estimates, there was a 75% drop in war-related deaths between the first and second half of the 20th century; most of

the deaths in the second half of the 20th century were civilian deaths.[199]

- After the Second World War, major international institutions came into being providing legally recognized forums for the prosecution of war criminals, the arbitration of disputes between nations, the development of international trade agreements and associations, the disbursement of international aid, the coordination of the eradication of diseases, and the maintenance and use of peace-keeping forces, among other areas.

One hundred years after 1912, these developments are astonishing in that war between nations has become unacceptable by international law and by the demands of the interdependent worldwide market economy. References to an 'international community' have become the norm, and several times, this 'community' has worked together to prevent conflict or the slaughter of civilians.

Many people, especially women, still suffer greatly because of civil war, insurgencies and terrorism. But one can reasonably say that by the early 21st century, peace between nations has broken out.

Chapter 6

'Abdu'l-Bahá:
Teacher, Sage and Pastor

Portrait of 'Abdu'l-Bahá by Juliet Thiompson

IN THE weeks after the Lake Mohonk Conference, 'Abdu'l-Bahá spoke in depth about the working of the spiritual world—the Nature of God and the Manifestations of God, the Reality of Man, and the Holy Spirit's movement through the world.

In these talks 'Abdu'l-Bahá spoke of "reality", only rarely using the word "truth". Reality is simply what it is and, as people look into reality, they find that the underlying reality is one. So as people study reality, they move closer to realizing their oneness as physical and spiritual beings: "… reality must be investigated; for reality is one, and by investigating it all will find love and unity".[200]

God is the transcendent and unknowable reality from which all existence flows:

> The Fatherhood of God, His loving-kindness and beneficence are apparent to all. In His mercy He provides fully and amply for His creatures, and if any soul sins, He does not suspend His bounty. All created things are visible manifestations of His Fatherhood, mercy and heavenly bestowals.[201]

(Talk at the reception at the Metropolitan Temple, May 28th)

> God is eternal and ancient—not a new God… The sovereignty, power, names and attributes of God are eternal, ancient. His names presuppose creation and predicate His existence and will. We say God is Creator. This name Creator appears when we connote creation. We say God is the Provider. This name presupposes and proves the existence of the provided. God is Love.[202]

(Talk at the Theosophical Lodge, May 30th)

Human beings are limited and dependent compared to the Divine Reality which is unlimited and independent.[203] So God Manifests Himself in human form—the person of the Manifestation of God—in whom all the Divine Attributes are reflected. This Manifestation of God is like a perfect mirror reflecting the Sun which is God; 'Abdu'l-Bahá sometimes described God as the "Sun of Reality".

'Abdu'l-Bahá wrote of Jesus, who was a Manifestation of God:

> Consider the statement recorded in the first chapter of the book of John: "In the beginning was the Word, and the Word was with God, and the Word was God." This statement is brief but replete with the greatest meanings… Heretofore the doctors of theology have not expounded it but have restricted it to Jesus as "the Word made flesh," the separation of Jesus from God, the Father, and His descent upon the earth. In this way the individualized separation of the godhead came to be taught. The essential oneness of Father, Son and Spirit has many meanings and constitutes the foundation

of Christianity. Today we will merely give a synopsis of explanation. Why was Jesus the Word? In the universe of creation all phenomenal beings are as letters. Letters in themselves are meaningless and express nothing of thought or ideal—as, for instance, a, b, etc. Likewise, all phenomenal beings are without independent meaning. But a word is composed of letters and has independent sense and meaning. Therefore, as Christ conveyed the perfect meaning of divine reality and embodied independent significance, He was the Word. He was as the station of reality compared to the station of metaphor. There is no intrinsic meaning in the leaves of a book, but the thought they convey leads you to reflect upon reality. The reality of Jesus was the perfect meaning, the Christhood in Him which in the Holy Books is symbolized as the Word.

"The Word was with God." The Christhood means not the body of Jesus but the perfection of divine virtues manifest in Him. Therefore, it is written, "He is God." This does not imply separation from God, even as it is not possible to separate the rays of the sun from the sun. The reality of Christ was the embodiment of divine virtues and attributes of God. For in Divinity there is no duality…[204]

(Talk at the Kinney home, May 29th)

A person comes nearer to God by striving to develop spiritual qualities:

Nearness to God is dependent upon purity of the heart and exhilaration of the spirit through the glad tidings of the Kingdom. Consider how a pure, well-polished mirror fully reflects the effulgence of the sun, no matter how distant the sun may be. As soon as the mirror is cleaned and purified, the sun will manifest itself. The more pure and sanctified the heart of man becomes, the nearer it draws to God, and the light of the Sun of Reality is revealed within it.[205]

Therefore, we learn that nearness to God is possible through devotion to Him, through entrance into the Kingdom and service to humanity; it is attained by unity with mankind and through loving-kindness to all; it is dependent upon investigation of truth, acquisition of praiseworthy virtues, service in the cause of universal peace and personal sanctification. In a word, nearness to God necessitates sacrifice of self, severance and the giving up of all to Him. Nearness is likeness.[206]

(Talk at the Mount Morris Baptist Church, May 26th)

Without developing these spiritual capacities, a human being will remain in the dark:

> Behold how the sun shines upon all creation, but only surfaces that are pure and polished can reflect its glory and light. The darkened soul has no portion of the revelation of the glorious effulgence of reality; and the soil of self, unable to take advantage of that light, does not produce growth. The eyes of the blind cannot behold the rays of the sun; only pure eyes with sound and perfect sight can receive them.[207]
>
> *(Talk at the Mount Morris Baptist Church, May 26th)*

> ...we must ever strive for capacity and seek readiness. As long as we lack susceptibility, the beauties and bounties of God cannot penetrate. Christ spoke a parable in which He said His words were like the seeds of the sower; some fall upon stony ground, some upon sterile soil, some are choked by thorns and thistles, but some fall upon the ready, receptive and fertile ground of human hearts. When seeds are cast upon sterile soil, no growth follows. Those cast upon stony ground will grow a short time, but lacking deep roots will wither away. Thorns and thistles destroy others completely, but the seed cast in good ground brings forth harvest and fruitage. In the same way, the words I speak to you here tonight may produce no effect whatever.[208]
>
> *(Talk at the Mount Morris Baptist Church, May 26th)*

The Manifestations of God have all been the perfect reflections of the Divine Reality and, since Reality is One, have all been united in purpose and essence:

> The divine Manifestations since the day of Adam have striven to unite humanity so that all may be accounted as one soul. The function and purpose of a shepherd is to gather and not disperse his flock. The Prophets of God have been divine Shepherds of humanity. They have established a bond of love and unity among mankind, made scattered peoples one nation and wandering tribes a mighty kingdom. They have laid the foundation of the oneness of God and summoned all to universal peace. All these holy, divine Manifestations are one. They have served one God, promulgated the same truth, founded the same institutions and reflected the same light. Their appearances have been successive and correlated; each One has announced and extolled the One Who was to follow, and all laid the foundation of reality.[209]
>
> *(Talk at the reception at the Metropolitan Temple, May 28th)*

Religious forms are man's living response to the Manifestation of God but attachment to a particular form of religion brings about imitation and man-made traditions and obscures the light of reality:

> Imitation destroys the foundation of religion, extinguishes the spirituality of the human world, transforms heavenly illumination into darkness and deprives man of the knowledge of God. It is the

cause of the victory of materialism and infidelity over religion; it is the denial of Divinity and the law of revelation; it refuses Prophethood and rejects the Kingdom of God.[210]

(Talk at Town Hall, Fanwood, NJ, May 31st)

Likewise, the divine religions of the holy Manifestations of God are in reality one, though in name and nomenclature they differ. Man must be a lover of the light, no matter from what dayspring it may appear. He must be a lover of the rose, no matter in what soil it may be growing. He must be a seeker of the truth, no matter from what source it come. Attachment to the lantern is not loving the light.[211]

(Talk at the reception at the Metropolitan Temple, May 28th)

Religion has two aspects:

The first is essential. It concerns morality and development of the virtues of the human world. This aspect is common to all. It is fundamental; it is one; there is no difference, no variation in it. As regards the inculcation of morality and the development of human virtues, there is no difference whatsoever between the teachings of Zoroaster, Jesus and Bahá'u'lláh. In this they agree; they are one. The second aspect of the divine religions is nonessential. It concerns human needs and undergoes change in every cycle according to the exigency of the time.[212]

(Talk at the Church of the Ascension, June 2nd)

While buildings such as churches and synagogues are centers where people can gather, the "…real Collective Centers are the Manifestations of God … the real divine temple and Collective Center of which the outer church is but a symbol"[213] and that, "Today Bahá'u'lláh is the Collective Center of unity for all mankind".[214]

While there are many different religions in outward form, "Bahá'u'lláh taught that reality is one and not multiple, that it underlies all precepts and that the foundations of the religions are, therefore, the same".[215]

But the seeker must differentiate between the lamp and the light, tradition and truth, and would have to "investigate reality" where he would find that "the foundation of the divine religions is reality; were there no reality, there would be no religions".[216] The seeker would then see that the multiplicity of religions is an illusion created by traditions, prejudice and blind imitation. At his talk at the Central Congregational Church in Brooklyn on June 16th, he illustrated this point by explaining that in the Qur'an, Muhammad asserts the Truth of Jesus's Mission and scolds His own followers for not having been followers of Jesus.[217]

Religion was also more than the salvation of individuals, it was the salvation of the world:

> The time has come when all mankind shall be united, when all races shall be loyal to one fatherland, all religions become one religion, and racial and religious bias pass away. It is a day in which the oneness of humankind shall uplift its standard and international peace, like the true morning, flood the world with its light.[218]
>
> *(Talk at the Theosophical Lodge, May 30th)*

> Tonight I am very happy in the realization that our aims and purposes are the same, our desires and longings are one. This is a reflection and evidence of the oneness of the world of humanity and the intention toward accomplishment of the Most Great Peace… In the world of existence there are no greater questions than these.[219]
>
> *(Talk at the Theosophical Lodge, May 30th)*

> …we must lay aside all prejudice—whether it be religious, racial, political or patriotic; we must become the cause of the unification of the human race. Strive for universal peace, seek the means of love, and destroy the basis of disagreement so that this material world may become divine, the world of matter become the realm of the Kingdom and humanity attain to the world of perfection.[220]
>
> *(Talk at Town Hall, Fanwood, NJ, May 31st)*

Bringing this peace, this great unification about would require "knowledge, volition and action"[221] on the part of individuals aided by the Power of God circulating throughout creation:

> In the same manner the bestowals of God are moving and circulating throughout all created things. This illimitable divine bounty has no beginning and will have no ending. It is moving, circulating and becomes effective wherever capacity is developed to receive it. In every station there is a specialized capacity. Therefore, we must be hopeful that through the bounty and favor of God this spirit of life infusing all created beings shall quicken humanity, and from its bestowals the human world shall become a divine world, …[222]
>
> *(Talk at the Theosophical Lodge, May 30th)*

> Consider how nothing but a spiritual power can bring about this unification, for material conditions and mental aspects are so widely different that agreement and unity are not possible through outer means. It is possible, however, for all to become unified through one spirit, just as all may receive light from one sun. Therefore, assisted by the collective and divine center which is the law of God and the

reality of His Manifestation, we can overcome these conditions until they pass away entirely and the races advance.[223]

(Talk at the Church of the Ascension, June 2nd)

The Manifestations of God, having both a human and a Divine Reality, know what humanity needs:

> The world of humanity may be likened to the individual man himself; it has its illness and ailments. A patient must be diagnosed by a skillful physician. The Prophets of God are the real Physicians. In whatever age or time They appear They prescribe for human conditions. They know the sicknesses; They discover the hidden sources of disease and indicate the necessary remedy… In this present age the world of humanity is afflicted with severe sicknesses and grave disorders which threaten death. Therefore, Bahá'u'lláh has appeared.[224]

(Talk at Kinney home, June 17th)

The ailment afflicting humanity in this day is "lack of love and absence of altruism".[225] This would be healed if "… the friends of God must adhere to the power which will create this love and unity in the hearts of the sons of men …"[226] because "… the spiritual teachings of the Religion of God can alone create this love, unity and accord in human hearts".[227]

In these talks of May/June 1912 and others, 'Abdu'l-Bahá laid out an entirely new vision of religion, one which freed the Divine Teachings from the man-made forms in which they had become trapped. He acknowledged the religious forms of the past while challenging the listener with the claim that these outward forms were transitory and that a new Divine Revelation had appeared—that God was alive and that His Spirit was moving in the world. This can be seen in 'Abdu'l-Bahá's explanation of the Divine Reality of Jesus which allowed the Christian to hold on to the Divinity of Jesus while being able to consider that the Christ-Spirit had returned in the human figure of Bahá'u'lláh. And while 'Abdu'l-Bahá challenged Christians and others, he never belittled the value of the work of their churches and organizations.

As a teacher, 'Abdu'l-Bahá spoke in a straightforward manner using simple metaphors and analogies to explain deeper truths. He used different approaches depending on the audience to which he spoke and used these approaches as bridges over which the listeners could cross into a deeper understanding of Bahá'u'lláh's Revelation. When he spoke at the Brotherhood Church in Jersey City, NJ, a non-denominational church organized by Howard Colby Ives who was a Unitarian minister, 'Abdu'l-Bahá focused on the meaning of true brotherhood. Then he used that to show how Bahá'u'lláh had caused true brotherhood between His followers and the importance of spiritual over material bonds. To the Theosophical Society, which believed that humans were parts of a spiritual whole and could improve through conscious awareness, he spoke of the ability of people to advance spiritually through "knowledge, volition, and action"[228] when aided by the Divine Power. At the Church of the Ascension on June 2nd, he began by speaking about the church building as a center for unity, and then he compared this kind of center of unity to the person of the Manifestation of God who was the collective center for the unification of the whole human race.

In these weeks after the Lake Mohonk Conference, the Master also made important predictions and statements about the future. During a rare question and answer session at the Church of the Ascension on June 2nd, 'Abdu'l-Bahá suggested that "the United States may be held up as the example of future government—that is to say, each province will be independent in itself, but there will be federal union protecting the interests of the various independent states",[229] and that "to cast aside centralization which promotes despotism is the exigency of the time";[230] despotism had been the history of the Kingdoms of the Near East including Persia—in the early 1900's the verb 'to elect' did not even exist in the Persian language.[231] He also asserted emphatically that woman's suffrage was key to the establishment of international peace.[232] The movement for woman's suffrage paralleled the lifespan of 'Abdu'l-Bahá: the women's movement began officially at the Seneca Falls Convention in 1848 and the constitutional amendment guaranteeing women the right to vote was passed in 1920, not long before the ascension of 'Abdu'l-Bahá. At this same question and answer session, someone asked the extraordinary question, "What will be the food of the united people?"[233] The Master answered that in time people would eat less meat and more grain as this is what human bodies had been designed to do.[234] On the evening of June 11th at 309 West 78th St., while stressing the primary importance of the spiritual life, 'Abdu'l-Bahá also emphasized the moral necessity and value of work:

> In this great Cause the light of guidance is shining and radiant. Bahá'u'lláh has even said that occupation and labor are devotion. All humanity must obtain a livelihood by sweat of the brow and bodily exertion, at the same time seeking to lift the burden of others, striving to be the source of comfort to souls and facilitating the means of living. This in itself is devotion to God. Bahá'u'lláh has thereby encouraged action and stimulated service. But the energies of the heart must not be attached to these things; the soul must not

be completely occupied with them. Though the mind is busy, the heart must be attracted toward the Kingdom of God in order that the virtues of humanity may be attained from every direction and source.²³⁵

(Talk at 309 West Seventy-Eighth Street, New York, June 11th)

Issues concerning labor—safety, pay, hours, working conditions, child labor—were very important social issues in the early 1900's, especially in a place like New York City with its millions of workers, many of them unskilled.

All of 'Abdu'l-Bahá's talks were for both the general public and the Bahá'ís; the Master made no distinction when teaching. At the same time, there was a core of believers who made up the "Bahá'í community", who were trying to organize themselves to spread the Bahá'í teachings.

The organization of the Bahá'í community in New York City began in 1900 with the arrival of the first Persian Bahá'í teacher to come to the United States, 'Abdu'l-Karím-i-Tihrání. He was sent by 'Abdu'l-Bahá to North America for the purposes of "spreading unison and agreement".²³⁶ The Faith had originally been brought to the United States by Ibráhím Kheiralla but this teacher had been spreading his own ideas mixed in with Bahá'í teachings. He eventually disobeyed 'Abdu'l-Bahá outright, which led to a fracturing of the American Bahá'í community with many leaving the Faith altogether. Tihrání, with the help of Howard MacNutt and Anton Haddad, drafted a set of "rules and laws" for the governance of the community which were then sent to the Master for approval.²³⁷

A Board of Counsel was elected on December 7th, 1900. The Bahá'ís chose as members Arthur P. Dodge, Hooper Harris, William H. Hoar, Andrew Hutchinson, Howard MacNutt, Frank E. Osborne, Edwin A. Putnam, Charles E. Sprague, and Orosco C. Woolson. All the members were male because of a misunderstanding of the passages in Bahá'u'lláh's Book of Laws referring to the membership of the House of Justice.²³⁸ For a whole decade, the Board lacked unity due to personality conflicts* and varying understandings of the Bahá'í teachings. This disunity rendered it much less effective than the Bahá'í administrative body in Chicago called the 'House of Spirituality'. The Board did manage to hold regular meetings but how the community grew and

---

*   See p. 10 above

how it was consolidated are unknown due to a lack of records, a result of the disagreements among the men. The members of the Board in New York City were highly educated making it harder for them to give up their own ideas. After the resignation of Arthur P. Dodge, one of its most prominent members, 'Abdu'l-Bahá wrote to him:

> There can be no greater harm for the Cause of God today than disunion, however small it may be! Consequently exert yourself to the utmost to gladden the hearts and to be the channel of fragrance and joy to mankind … [show] to the whole human race the utmost kindness; then how much more you must be kind to the spiritual friends [Bahá'ís]![239]

Though women did not serve on the Board, Gertrude Harris, the wife of Hooper Harris, helped organize the women into a 'Bahá'í Unity League for Ladies'[240] Women such as Gertrude Harris, Juliet Thompon, Isabella Brittingham, Marjorie Morten, Lua Getsinger, among many others, played a very active role in the development of the community.

The Bahá'ís met and the community's life developed. Feasts were held regularly and included friends of the Faith.[241] The Bahá'ís celebrated a Holy Day in honor of 'Abdu'l-Bahá called the "Feast of the Master", the Day of the Covenant.[242] They gathered for worship on Sundays:

> … as I entered the Assembly singing 'Onward Christian Soldiers', a song I always loved. It is stirring and inspires hope and courage. Here I was impressed by the wonderful love among the believers. What a contrast to the world of strife and commotion without![243]

Circular letters went out to community members of which it is estimated there were about one-hundred.[244] The Board and two other small groups of believers in the City published materials on the Faith early on, and there were funds and experienced writers and publishers in the community but the disunity hampered the publishing effort.[245] The New York Community even decided to write to 'Abdu'l-Bahá in March of 1908, for permission to begin a Temple fund to raise "funds for the purchase of a suitable headquarters for our assembly in the city of New York",[246] to which 'Abdu'l-Bahá replied that, "In the future, God Willing, there will be erected throughout all the regions of America—and, in particular, in New York—temples of outstanding beauty and dignity … For the present, however, be ye content with a rented property".[247]

The disunity which affected the New York Baha'is continued, such that by 1909 a younger group of believers was actively seeking to change the membership of the Board of Counsel. The believers had no knowledge or guidance on how to conduct Bahá'í elections. Several active believers who were not re-elected, such as Howard McNutt, started a Board of Counsel in Brooklyn, the Borough in which they lived. The 1910 elections saw another great turnover in membership. To try to unify the believers, 'Abdu'l-Bahá wrote to them and told them to expand the membership of the Board to twenty-seven members. The Master wanted all the different factions in the community to be included thereby helping them resolve their differences. This time, He instructed them to include women; Isabella Brittingham was elected the secretary, and she wrote to the Master to let him know that the elections had been harmonious. At this time, the Board changed its title to reflect the Master's use of 'mahfil-i-rawhání' when referring to consultative bodies. The Board would now be called by that title; it meant 'Spiritual Assembly'.

On the evening of June 12th, 'Abdu'l-Bahá met with the Assembly*. Juliet Thompson described Board meetings as "deadly".[248] 'Abdu'l-Bahá provided them with the metaphor of the telegraph by which the members could guide the spirit of their consultations. Knowing that the illness of the believers in New York City was disunity, 'Abdu'l-Bahá prescribed the remedy which was unity achieved through the investigation of reality coupled with an individual commitment to love of God over love of self:

> It is my hope that the meetings of the Bahá'í Assembly in New York shall become like meetings of the Supreme Concourse. When you assemble, you must reflect the lights of the heavenly Kingdom. Let your hearts be as mirrors in which the radiance of the Sun of Reality is visible. Each bosom must be a telegraph station—one terminus of the wire attached to the soul, the other fixed in the Supreme Concourse—so that inspiration may descend from the Kingdom of Abhá and questions of reality be discussed. Then opinions will coincide with truth; day by day there will be progression, and the meetings will become more radiant and spiritual. This attainment is conditioned upon unity and agreement. The more perfect the love and agreement, the more the divine confirmations and assistance of the Blessed Perfection will descend. May this prove to be a divine meeting, and may boundless bestowals come down upon you. Strive with all your hearts and with the very power of life that unity and love may continually increase. In discussions look toward the reality without being self-opinionated. Let no one assert and insist upon his

---

*   In the *Promulgation of Universal Peace*, the Board of Counsel is referenced as the 'Open committee'. The title 'Spiritual Assembly' was also now in use. These three titles refer to the same thing at this time.

own mere opinion; nay, rather, let each investigate reality with the greatest love and fellowship. Consult upon every matter, and when one presents the point of view of reality itself, that shall be acceptable to all. Then will spiritual unity increase among you, individual illumination will be greater, happiness will be more abundant, and you will draw nearer and nearer to the Kingdom of God.[249]

Chapter 7

"I am the Covenant"

Center of the Covenant

MANY OF the early American Bahá'ís were steeped in Christianity; the Faith was first taught in the 1890's as the fulfillment of Biblical prophecy. It was not unusual for Bahá'ís to continue to be involved in their churches. Hymns were a regular part of any worship. By the 1900's American Bahá'ís generally approached the Faith in two different ways. One group understood sacred scripture to be the absolute and only standard for knowing and understanding truth. The other group—especially prominent in the case of New York City—were people who tended to have highly developed personal ideas regarding society, spiritual truth, and politics, and who emphasized their own personal experience as a guide to belief rather than scripture or church. The New York Bahá'ís were made up of successful businessmen, artists, and writers, who tended to have this kind of confidence in their own views. These Bahá'ís held numerous beliefs that were 'alternatives' to church teaching, Biblical teaching, and the Bahá'í Writings, with which many were not yet familiar since few Writings were actually available to them.[250]

Among these beliefs was reincarnation, which had been taught by Ibráhím Kheiralla and which interested other believers who had studied Hinduism on their own. Thornton Chase, the first American Bahá'í, had believed in reincarnation prior to being corrected by 'Abdu'l-Bahá; Chase was very obedient to the Master and was able to let this belief go. Chase's letters, though, show that many other Bahá'ís continued to believe in reincarnation.[251] Howard MacNutt had been very interested in Hinduism and, even after becoming a Bahá'í, he tended to combine his understandings of Hinduism with the Bahá'í teachings. For example, he taught that Bahá'u'lláh would bring unity in the world by blending religions together and, in his book, Unity Through Love, he put forth pantheistic beliefs that God is in nature and imminent in humanity, meaning the Divine Will would appear in the human soul.[252] As a result of this inaccurate description of the Bahá'í Teachings, few of his talks were recorded or printed. Over time, there were fewer requests for him to speak publicly about the Faith. Of course, MacNutt was expressing his own understanding and meant no malice, nor did he intend to distort the teachings of the Faith which he loved deeply.[253]

In another example of alternative beliefs among Bahá'ís, Charles Mason Remey remembered an active Bahá'í in New York City who told people that 'Abdu'l-Bahá was sending her tablets by telepathy; she continued to say this until 'Abdu'l-Bahá arrived in New York City and told her to stop.[254] Percy Woodcock, one of the most active New York

Bahá'ís, was fascinated by astrology, asceticism, and Egyptian pyramids; he believed that the building of a House of Worship would attract the ancient power of the pyramids. This presented a challenge to the Board especially as Percy was a well-liked teacher of the Faith.[255] Isabella Brittingham had to give a talk multiple times around 1905 entitled "The Phenomenal World" to counter prevalent beliefs in psychics among Bahá'ís. She taught that psychic powers existed but were different from the spiritual perceptions which lead one nearer to God, and that spiritual growth came from knowledge of Bahá'u'lláh as the Manifestation of God, obedience to the Divine Laws, and service to others, exactly as 'Abdu'l-Bahá had taught.[256]

Believers like Isabella Brittingham helped the Bahá'ís gain a truer understanding of the Faith. She descended from an old American family that included a signer of the Declaration of Independence. Deeply rooted in Biblical prophecy, she became a Bahá'í in 1898, after coming to believe that the Bible had predicted the coming of Bahá'u'lláh in symbolic terms. She made a first pilgrimage to 'Abdu'l-Bahá in 'Akká in September, 1904, after the Master had been incarcerated again in the 'Akká prison, and a second in 1909. She became an ardent teacher of the Faith and traveled with the support of her husband James, also a devout Bahá'í. Beginning in March of 1910, she served on the Unity Board whose members were to correspond with Women's Assemblies of the Orient. Dr. Susan Moody, a believer whom Isabella had deepened, and her niece, Elizabeth Stewart, moved to Iran where they founded a medical practice for the poor.[257] Isabella wrote an essay, "The Revelation of Bahá'u'lláh", that contained accurate descriptions of the Bahá'í Teachings, including the Station of 'Abdu'l-Bahá. She described the station of the Master as being the Center of the Covenant, "He who knows no station save that of servitude, humility, and lowliness to the Beloved of El-Baha".[258]

The station of 'Abdu'l-Bahá was the central point about which Bahá'ís in New York City were unclear. Even a believer as experienced as Edward Getsinger, who had been to 'Akká three times for a total of six months and who had listened to 'Abdu'l-Bahá numerous times as well as having studied with numerous Persian teachers, continued to equate 'Abdu'l-Bahá as "The Christ of this generation to the Gentiles, and not what He in His humility chooses to claim for Himself – a servant".[259]

Arthur P. Dodge's main orientation was as someone who was anti-church; he saw the churches and Christian beliefs as hopelessly corrupted. 'Abdu'l-Bahá, for him, was the returned Christ who would re-infuse religion with a true spirit. Dodge was a man with a wide array of talents despite his limited education. Early in life he had been a drummer boy in his father's Union regiment in the Civil War. He had become a reporter at the age of sixteen, a self-taught lawyer, a publisher who dreamed of publishing a national magazine to educate the masses, and a mechanical engineer who designed engines and built a company with valuable patents. He married Elizabeth Day with whom he had six children. He first heard of the Faith through his father in 1895 who had been told of it by Dr. Sarah J. Burgess. His father was in deep grief over the loss of his daughter, Anna, and was very receptive to the teachings which helped him weather his bereavement. Dodge and his wife took Kheiralla's entire series of lessons when they were given in New York City, and he became a devoted lifelong teacher of the Faith. He was elected the first 'president of the New York Bahá'ís in 1898, went on pilgrimage to 'Akká with his wife and two sons in 1900, and, in 1901, he wrote and published the first introductory book on the Bahá'í Faith by a Western believer, *The Truth of It: The Inseparable Oneness of Common Sense—Science—Religion*. Much of this book, however, was an attack on the clergy, the corruption of organized religion, and scientists.[260] When there were personality clashes with Dodge among the Bahá'ís in New York City, 'Abdu'l-Bahá wrote to them:

> This personage is a believer and assured; he is attracted, enkindled and of the utmost sincerity. The believers of God must have the utmost consideration toward him; they must not avoid him; they must seek his companionship in a cheerful manner… The point is this: the believers must associate with Mr. Dodge with joy and love.[261]

Dodge later served as a delegate in 1912 and 1913 to the Bahá'í Temple Unity Conventions. In his later years he moved to Long Island and helped found the community of Hempstead. His faith helped to reduce his anger towards the churches.[262]

'Abdu'l-Karim Tihrání, a Persian teacher, had a book published in 1900 that contained his talks in Chicago, Kenosha and New York City, *Addresses by Abdel Karim Effendi Teherani: Delivered before the New York and Chicago Assemblies*. The talks focused on the importance of obedience to the Covenant of Bahá'u'lláh, and he calls 'Abdu'l-Bahá the 'Center of the Covenant' fifty-four times in these talks. All of this was to counter the problems that had arisen from the false teachings of Kheiralla and his disobedience to the Master. This publication was the first time American Bahá'ís were hearing the term and concept of a 'Covenant breaker'.[263]

Though Tihrání had not spent much time in New York City, the City was a transit point for pilgrims going to and from 'Akká who, on their return, told the believers what they had heard directly from the Master. These talks and notes by pilgrims were a rich source for understanding the Faith though, in time, they would not be considered authoritative. In the Autumn of 1900, the Getsingers, the Dodges, and the Hoars made a pilgrimage to 'Akká. There, they learned directly from 'Abdu'l-Bahá the true Bahá'í teachings, dispelling erroneous notions spread by Kheiralla—most shockingly, that Bahá'u'lláh did not teach the reincarnation of souls. When the pilgrims returned, Dodge published a compilation of Bahá'í Writings and tablets they had received from 'Abdu'l-Bahá, Tablets from Abdul Beha Abbas to Some American Believers in the year 1900.[264] His sons, William Copeland Dodge and Wendell Phillips Dodge published in 1901, Utterances of Abdul Beha Abbas to two young men, American pilgrims in Acre, 1901.[265]

In November, 1900, after the pilgrims had returned, two Persian teachers Mírzá Asadu'lláh and Hájí Hasan-i-Khurásání and two translators arrived to deepen Bahá'ís. Asadu'lláh was one of 'Abdu'l-Bahá's most trusted assistants—he had been given the sacred task of transporting the remains of the Báb from Iran to the Holy Land. These Persian teachers were instrumental in helping the New York Bahá'ís form the Board of Counsel, though they were not able to stay long enough to correct the ideas left by Kheiralla's false teachings.[266]

Another Persian teacher who introduced more of the Bahá'í Teachings to American believers was Anton Haddad. During 1901 and 1902, he wrote and published several works. In The Maxim of Bahaism, he explained the necessity for a new Manifestation, and he made a fifty-three point summary of the Laws contained in Bahá'u'lláh's Book of Laws. In The Station of the Manifestation and the Greatness of this Day, he showed that the coming of Bahá'u'lláh was the cause of the many advances in their time and that science was inherently in agreement with religion. Lastly, in Divine Revelation the Basis of All Civilization, he endeavored to show that Divine Revelation was the source and motive power of human and social progress, and he quoted directly from Bahá'u'lláh's Book of Laws and His "Words of Wisdom".[267]

In 1901, the finest scholar in the Bahá'í world, Mírzá Abu'l-Fazl, arrived in the United States. He was fifty-seven by then, frail of health, and found himself in cold climates for the first time; he had left behind in Egypt his library, students, and scholarly resources. Abu'l-Fazl wrote a book for the American believers, The Bahá'í Proofs. In this profound work, he included biographies of the Central Figures of the Faith, a summary of the history of the Faith to 1900, detailed comparisons between the Bahá'í Faith and the Abrahamic Faiths, an explanation of Bahá'u'lláh's teachings in terms of God's relationship to man, man's relationship to himself, and God's relationship to society. He also made a short list of Bahá'u'lláh's social principles, and wrote introductions of four other religions asked for by 'Abdu'l-Bahá. Abu'l Fazl spent most his time in the United States in Washington DC. *The Bahá'í Proofs* was a highly sophisticated, closely reasoned source, the likes of which Americans had not read before. Most likely, the Americans were not able to appreciate its depths; Abu'l-Fazl used his extensive knowledge of Bahá'í Scripture, Aristotelian logic, Arabic, Persian, and Islamic theology and history, while Americans were asking him to interpret their dreams. Over the course of the 20th century, it was the only book from the early part of the century to be reprinted.[268]

Even with these explanations of the Station of 'Abdu'l-Bahá, there continued to be differences on this subject among the believers. In 1907, 'Abdu'l-Bahá wrote to the Consultative Assembly of New York and both clarified the Station of Bahá'u'lláh and the Báb as being that of the Returned Christ and elevated Servitude to the Highest Station:

> You have written that there is a difference among the believers concerning the 'Second Coming of Christ'. Gracious God! Time and again this question hath arisen, and its answer hath emanated in a clear and irrefutable statement from the pen of 'Abdu'l-Bahá, that what is meant in the prophecies by the 'Lord of Hosts' and the 'Promised Christ' is the Blessed Perfection [Bahá'u'lláh] and His Holiness the Exalted One [the Báb]. This clear and irrefutable statement must provide, for all, the foundation of their belief. My name is 'Abdu'l-Bahá. My qualification is 'Abdu'l-Bahá. My reality is 'Abdu'l-Bahá. My praise is 'Abdu'l-Bahá. Thraldom to the Blessed Perfection is my glorious and refulgent diadem, and servitude to all the human race my perpetual religion … No name, no title, no mention, no commendation have I, nor will ever have, except 'Abdu'l-Bahá. This is my longing. This is my greatest yearning. This is my eternal life. This is my everlasting glory … O Friends of God! 'Abdu'l-Bahá is not the return of Christ, but the very embodiment of servitude.[269]

It is hundreds of Tablets like this that provided the American believers with their greatest source of knowledge concerning the true Bahá'í Teachings and for understanding what it meant to live a Bahá'í life. The tablets were translated, typed, and mailed to Bahá'í communities and exchanged between communities and individuals so that they provided a steady source of infallible guidance. It is important for posterity to remember that these tablets were written by 'Abdu'l-Bahá in response to specific questions asked by the believers, so the subjects of the Tablets represented the interests of the questioners. These tablets do not represent an effort by 'Abdu'l-Bahá to give a systematic theology of Bahá'u'lláh's Revelation; much of the Master's guidance was pastoral—how people could live together in communities or which virtues were important, for example—as he sought to instruct the believers in how to live a Bahá'í life both individually and collectively. These tablets should be understood in this context.

In a July, 1912, edition of the *Star of the West,* a bi-monthly publication about the Faith, Charles Mason Remey explained the Station of 'Abdu'l-Bahá to the readers:

> 'Abdu'l-Bahá's life of service is the Center of the life of the Kingdom which is the Bahá'í Cause. His servitude to God and service to mankind is the heart from which the life force of the Kingdom is flowing to all the members of that growing spiritual body. He is the interpreter and the expounder of Holy Writ. BAHA'O'LLAH commanded all to turn to 'Abdu'l-Bahá, who is the Greatest Branch – branched from the Pre-existent Root – the Center of the Covenant of God.[270]

That same edition of *Star of the West* included a tablet from 'Abdu'l-Bahá to Mason Remey on the subject of the Covenant:

> Likewise with the trace of the Supreme Pen He (Bahá'u'lláh) has taken a Great Covenant and Testament after His Departure they must obey the Center of the Covenant and must not deviate one hair's breadth from obedience to him. He has commanded in the most explicit terms in two instances in the Book of Akdas and He has appointed most unmistakably the interpreter of the Book. In all Tablets, especially the chapter of "Branch," whose meanings are all 'Abdu'l-Bahá– that is, "the Servant of Baha" – everything that is necessary is revealed from the Supreme Pen. As 'Abdu'l-Bahá is the interpreter of the Book, he says that the chapter of "Branch" means 'Abdu'l-Bahá and nothing else.[271]

That summer, *The Bahá'í Proofs,* an essay by Abu'l Fazl, was published in the United States. In it, he explained 'Abdu'l-Bahá's station in clear and direct terms grounded in the Bahá'í Writings:

> To the people of Faith, the clear appointment of the Center of the Cause, after the Departure [Death] of the Manifestation [Baha'o'llah], is considered the most important point in religious matters, as it is the greatest channel which connects the servants of God with the Holy Divine Truth. They are all sure and convinced that the CENTER

OF THE COVENANT is no other than His Holiness, 'ABDU'L-BAHÁ; for, apart from the Divine signs that are manifest in Him, BAHA'O'LLAH clearly and implicitly, verbally and in writing, directed all of His servants to the blessed Person of 'ABDU'L-BAHÁ, and, under all circumstances, clearly showed that He was far distinguished above others, in order that all the servants should look unto Him alone, and follow His Commands. For it is only through His explanation and decision that all discord is removed... He prior to His Departure, revealed the Kitab-el-A'hd [Book of the Covenant, the Will of BAHA'O'LLAH]. This He wrote with His own blessed Hand and Seal, ... In this Book (His Covenant) He clearly indicated that the purpose of the "Branch extended from the Ancient Root," revealed in the blessed Verse of Akdas, was the Center of the Circle of Names, the Exalted Branch of the Blessed Tree of ABHA, His Holiness ABDUL-BAHA. Then He, for the second time, enjoined, through an unchangeable and irrefutable command, all His "branches," "twigs," (relatives) and the Bahá'ís without exception, to look unto that Dawning-Place of Divine Light, and to know Him as the Source and Origin of the commands and prohibitions of the Heavenly Religion.[272]

At the time, the *Star of the West* printed this encouragement by 'Abdu'l-Bahá concerning this work by Abu'l-Fazl:

> In reality, this treatise is the Sharp and Brilliant Proof which has emanated from the breath of the pen of servitude to the Blessed Perfection.[273]

In the same November edition of *Star of the West,* a talk by 'Abdu'l-Bahá was reprinted:

> His Holiness BAHA'O'LLAH covenanted, not that I ('Abdu'l-Bahá) am the Promised One, but that Abdul-Baha is the expounder of the Book and the CENTRE OF HIS COVENANT, and that the Promised One of BAHA'O'LLAH will appear after one thousand or thousands of years... In case of difference, 'Abdu'l-Bahá must be consulted... After "Abdu'l-Bahá, whenever the Universal House of Justice is organized it will ward off differences...[274]

That edition also printed Bahá'u'lláh's *Book of the Covenant,* which was Bahá'u'lláh's 'Will and Testament':

> "He hath forbidden dispute and strife with an absolute prohibition in the book (Kitab el-Akdas)... "This is the TESTAMENT OF GOD, that the Branches (Aghsan), Twigs (Afnan), and Relations (Muntessabeen), must each and every one look to the Greatest Branch (Ghusn Azam)...[275]

Mrs. Gibbons, a Bahá'í, had written the Master before his coming to the United States, requesting that her own daughter be allowed to paint his portrait. In his reply he consented to this request and added, according to Mrs. Gibbons, that Juliet Thompson would paint a portrait of him. Juliet Thompson had long dreamed that she would paint the face of Christ.[276]

During the month of June, 'Abdu'l-Bahá allowed Juliet Thompson to paint his portrait telling her to paint his "Servitude to God". She completed it over the course of six sittings which took place over multiple days in different rooms. Juliet remembered that fourth sitting on June 19th because of an extraordinary experience she and Lua Getsinger had on that day. As the Master prepared to sit for the portrait, he turned to Lua Getsinger who was also in the room and told her in Persian that these sittings made him sleepy. He sat down and closed his eyes. Juliet studied him but found that she could not begin painting because 'Abdu'l-Bahá's countenance reflected the dignity and peace of the Divine Realm.[277]

Then, as though awakened by the Holy Spirit, 'Abdu'l-Bahá opened his eyes and with great power said:

> I appoint you, Lua, the Herald of the Covenant. And I AM THE COVENANT, appointed by Bahá'u'lláh. And no one can refute His Word. This is the Testament of Bahá'u'lláh. You will find it in the Holy Book of Aqdas. Go forth and proclaim, 'This is THE COVENANT OF GOD in your midst.'[278]

A great joy seemed to fill Lua while Juliet wept at witnessing this extraordinary moment of spiritual force flowing through the Master. Then 'Abdu'l-Bahá became quiet again. The Holy Spirit receded, and 'Abdu'l-Bahá the man re-emerged. He smiled at Juliet and told her that she must stop crying since she would not be able to paint through tears.[279]

In the afternoon of that same day He sent Lua Getsinger downstairs to speak about the Covenant to the visitors waiting there.[280] When he went down later,* he read from Bahá'u'lláh's 'Tablet of the Branch' and spoke with great power on the Covenant.[281]

---

* In *Mahmoud's Diary*, Mahmoud states that 'Abdu'l-Bahá spoke about the 'Tablet of the Branch' at a "public meeting" but this meeting was not recorded in *Promulgation of Universal Peace*. Juliet Thompson's diary does not record 'Abdu'l-Bahá's talk to the visitors that day either. She writes "In the afternoon of that same day He sent Lua down to the waiting people to "proclaim the Covenant"; then a little later followed her and spoke Himself on the station of the Centre of the Covenant, but not as He had done to Lua and me. The blazing Reality of it He had revealed in His own Person to us. To them He spoke guardedly, even deleting afterwards from our notes some of the things He had said." These notes have not been preserved.

'Abdu'l-Bahá designated New York City, the 'City of the Covenant'.²⁸²

Differences of understanding about the Station of 'Abdu'l-Bahá would continue despite the numerous Tablets, notes from returning pilgrims, articles, reprints of talks, and translations of the Book of the Covenant and the Tablet of the branch in the *Star of the West,* until 1934, the year Shoghi Effendi wrote *The Dispensation of Bahá'u'lláh.* The *Dispensation* gave definitive explanations to Bahá'ís regarding the Natures and Stations of the Báb, Bahá'u'lláh, and 'Abdu'l-Bahá. Also, by the 1930's enough of a distinctive 'Baha'i way of life' had appeared so that the points in the *Dispensation* could be fully appreciated and would replace the personal opinions of believers.

Shoghi Effendi explained that 'Abdu'l-Bahá was not an ordinary man nor was he the Manifestation of God:

> For wide as is the gulf that separates 'Abdu'l-Bahá from Him Who is the Source of an independent Revelation, it can never be regarded as commensurate with the greater distance that stands between Him Who is the Center of the Covenant and His ministers who are to carry on His work, whatever be their name, their rank, their functions or their future achievements.²⁸³

'Abdu'l-Bahá was the 'Mystery of God' who functioned as the Center of the Covenant and perfect Exemplar, a guide for all believers:

> He is, and should for all time be regarded, first and foremost, as the Center and Pivot of Bahá'u'lláh's peerless and all-enfolding Covenant, His most exalted handiwork, the stainless Mirror of His light, the perfect Exemplar of His teachings, the unerring Interpreter of His Word, the embodiment of every Bahá'í ideal, the incarnation of every Bahá'í virtue, the Most Mighty Branch sprung from the Ancient Root, the Limb of the Law of God, the Being "round Whom all names revolve," the Mainspring of the Oneness of Humanity, the Ensign of the Most Great Peace, the Moon of the Central Orb of this most holy Dispensation—styles and titles that are implicit and find their truest, their highest and fairest expression in the magic name 'Abdu'l-Bahá. He is, above and beyond these appellations, the "Mystery of God"—an expression by which Bahá'u'lláh Himself has chosen to designate Him, and which, while it does not by any means justify us to assign to Him the station of Prophethood, indicates how in the person of 'Abdu'l-Bahá the incompatible characteristics of a human nature and superhuman knowledge and perfection have been blended and are completely harmonized.²⁸⁴

Chapter 8

The Unity Feast: New Jersey

Unity Feast in NEw Jersey

NEWSPAPERS AND visitors often described 'Abdu'l-Bahá with words such as "dignified", "Christ-like", "Divine"; those who were able to spend more time with him personally also experienced his emotional expressiveness and affection, his naturalness and spontaneity and his practical approach to living.

'Abdu'l-Bahá readily expressed his emotions from the welcoming smile with which he greeted people to laughter and, even, tears. For example, one Friday afternoon in July, Dr. Percy Grant came to visit 'Abdu'l-Bahá. Grant was in a combative mood possibly due to his jealousy over the devotion Juliet had to 'Abdu'l-Bahá. The Master greeted him with a warm welcome. As they spoke, Grant kept questioning and debating 'Abdu'l-Bahá at one point making a very emphatic point with, according to Juliet Thompson, the air of a victor. Rather than be offended or reactive, 'Abdu'l-Bahá burst out laughing and offered another point of view. Gradually, Grant's combativeness lessened when confronted by 'Abdu'l-Bahá's humble good humor.[285] One afternoon in Montclair, 'Abdu'l-Bahá retold the story of the martyrdom of 'Abdu'l-Vahháb-i-Shírází. As he remembered the suffering of this young martyr, the Master's entire countenance became ecstatic, and he began singing the "Martyr's song".[286] He felt sorrow keenly as well, especially when he thought of his Father. When the hotel manager asked him in early July if he would like a tour of the rest of the large hotel, he declined telling the believers:

> When I see magnificent buildings and beautiful scenery, I contrast them with memories of the prison and of the persecutions suffered by the Blessed Beauty and my heart is deeply moved and I seek to avoid such sightseeing excursions.[287]

'Abdu'l-Bahá was so genuinely affectionate that he was able to pierce through the barriers of social convention and touch people's hearts. When Howard Colby Ives began to shed tears during their first encounter, the master wiped these tears away with his own fingers. After Kate Carew, the hardened reporter, had finished her interview with him, he led her down the hall through the lobby while holding her hand—much to her astonishment. When Juliet Thompson's maid, Mamie, wanted her little boy, George, to be blessed by 'Abdu'l-Bahá, the Master picked up the little boy and without ceremony placed him on his knee and caressed and played with him; this boy went on to practice medicine.

The Master responded to people with open-hearted friendliness—the race, appearance, disposition, class or gender of a person made no difference whatever. He met two African American youth in early July and encouraged them in their spiritual lives, giving them Persian names—'Mubárak', for the man, 'Khush Ghadam', for the woman. Though the United States during these years was steeped in racial segregation, 'Abdu'l-Bahá disregarded these social conventions completely and actively set an example of inter-racial fellowship during his visit to Washington DC.[288] Another day in early July, he went out for a stroll and a Greek man came up to him and brought over his friends as well. The Master spoke to them about Greek philosophers and encouraged their own moral improvement.[289] On an especially hot July day, 'Abdu'l-Bahá had consented to visit the Natural History Museum. After the visit, he sat under a birch tree in an area where people were not supposed to sit. The elderly Jewish watchman who had let the Master's party in earlier approached and said he would like to meet 'Abdu'l-Bahá because he seemed like a great man. As the watchman approached him, the Master turned around, smiled and invited the elderly man to sit next to him. He replied that he couldn't because of the rules but that the Master could. So as to be able to speak with the elderly watchman, 'Abdu'l-Bahá stood up and turned to him.[290] In another incident, 'Abdu'l-Bahá was walking on the sidewalk towards the home of the Harrises on 95th St.. Many children were playing, jumping rope and hula hooping outside. When they saw 'Abdu'l-Bahá pass by, they all followed him with his powerful stride and long white robe and beard. Once the Master had gone into the building, the children all waited around the stoop, and Juliet Thompson spoke to them. Her friend Rhoda Nichols went inside to let 'Abdu'l-Bahá know what was happening out front. She returned with an invitation for the children to come the following night to the Kinneys for dinner.[291]

'Abdu'l-Bahá moved according to the spirit, and this made him very spontaneous. Edward Getsinger had to plan many of the Master's appointments, an exhausting job. Edward wrote to Agnes Parsons, a Bahá'í in Washington DC:

Now one more important thing: -

We have tried to have 'Abdu'l-Bahá say that he would for certain be your guest, but without avail. He said "I cannot be bound in any place or arrangement before the day arrives. The spirit arranges to set the contingencies." I said "then if you might want an apartment by yourself, it is best I write to have one found." He said "very well, but do not engage it, if I like it when I see it, I will choose it, if not, then I don't want it".[292]

And, in regards to a press conference in Washington DC, Edward wrote:

> I wrote the Turkish Ambassador before I left, leaving the presentation in abeyance, pending his arrival. 'Abdu'l-Bahá said "that if my presentation to the Press includes also my declaration of citizenship of any country, then I will decline, as I am a citizen of the world.[293]

Often, 'Abdu'l-Bahá enjoyed going to Riverside Park near his living quarters to simply lie down in the grass for a rest.[294] When a Greek friend asked him to come meet his friends in a park, they took the subway together, and 'Abdu'l-Bahá sat down in the grass and spoke to the friends as they approached him.[295] Though the Master was always polite, he was never mannered or pretentious. His comments and responses were always natural, truthful and heartfelt. When he met Admiral Peary on May 5th, at the Union League in Brooklyn, he offered this wonderfully nuanced praise according to Juliet Thompson:

> …for a very long time the world had been much concerned about the North Pole, where it was and what was to be found there. Now he, Admiral Peary, had discovered it and that nothing was to [be] found there; and so, in forever relieving the public mind, he had rendered a great service.[296]

As well as the sincere exhortation he gave him directly:

> I hope that you will raise the standard of universal peace.[297]

The Master also took a very hands-on approach to daily life. He met with group after group, and privately with many individuals, getting to know people, their questions and concerns, personally. He spent countless hours on letter writing. In June, he spoke of this to some Bahá'ís in Montclair, NJ:

> After the Ascension of Bahá'u'lláh I did everything within my power to promote the Cause of God. I clung to spiritual methods and rendered such servitude at the Threshold of God so that the divine Cause might advance throughout the world. And my correspondence was so heavy that, at the time of the death of an American maidservant of God, my letters to her were counted and numbered sixty-seven; so you can imagine the situation!

In late June, he moved to a house in Montclair, NJ, a suburb of New York City, to escape the city heat. He invited guests there and bought the food for them himself in the market, supervised its preparation and served it himself.[298]

Before leaving for New Jersey, 'Abdu'l-Bahá had invited the Bahá'ís in New York City for a unity feast to be held on June 29th at Roy Wilhelm's family home in West Englewood, NJ:

> I am about to leave the city for a few days rest at Montclair. When I return, it is my wish to give a large feast of unity... It must be outdoors under the trees, in some location away from city noise—like a Persian garden. The food will be Persian food. When the place is arranged, all will be informed, and we will have a general meeting in which hearts will be bound together, spirits blended and a new foundation for unity established. All the friends will come. They will be my guests. They will be as the parts and members of one body. The spirit of life manifest in that body will be one spirit. The foundation of that temple of unity will be one foundation. Each will be a stone in that foundation, solid and interdependent. Each will be as a leaf, blossom or fruit upon one tree. For the sake of fellowship and unity I desire this feast and spiritual gathering.[299]

The town of West Englewood later became Teaneck which gained the distinction of being the first town in the nation where a white majority voted for school integration.[300] Roy and his father lived in West Englewood and commuted daily to their coffee company's offices in the City.

Roy Wilhelm was born in Ohio, the Christian heartland of the United States. His grandmother, mother, and father were all seekers. They wanted to go beyond church doctrine and learn about new philosophies and religious thought. His grandmother especially sensed that they were living in a New Day, a 'Promised Day'. Roy's mother befriended a lady who lived nearby, Laura Jones, who was also on a spiritual search. When Jones moved to Chicago, she came into contact with Bahá'ís and sent Bahá'í pamphlets to Mrs. Wilhelm who straightaway became a believer after reading them. Roy was skeptical about his mother's conversion as she had been interested in many new religious ideas. While he continued his profession as a traveling salesmen for his father's coffee company, he also attended Bahá'í meetings in New York City. When the Dodges returned from a nine-day pilgrimage to 'Akká, they rented a home to which they invited seekers. Going to these gatherings, Roy became very attracted to the Faith though he knew only a little bit about its teachings. In 1907, he and his mother made a pilgrimage to 'Akká where they stayed in the prison with 'Abdu'l-Bahá for six days. Roy remembers:

> During our last meal 'Abdu'l-Bahá always broke a quantity of bread into His bowl; then asking for the plates of the pilgrims. He gave to

each of us a portion. When the meal was finished, He said: I have given you to eat from My bowl – now distribute My Bread among the people.[301]

Roy became a confirmed believer. He would go on to serve on the National Spiritual Assembly, on the editorial Board of Star of the West, and as a traveling teacher who also underwrote the efforts of others such as Martha Root. 'Abdu'l-Bahá placed great trust in Roy, writing to him, "The sight of your portrait brought joy to My heart, because it is luminous and celestial …"[302] The Master directed much mail for other believers to Roy. When Shoghi Effendi suddenly became the head of the Faith, he invited Roy, among other believers, to come to Haifa and consult with him about the Bahá'í world. He praised him for his "saintliness, indomitable faith, outstanding services …"[303]

The day of the unity feast came. Chairs for the guests had been set up in a circle under the evergreen trees. 'Abdu'l-Bahá, who that morning had ridden four trains in the June heat to get to West Englewood, entered the circle. A carpet of flowers covered the lawn. The air was pure, a breeze picked up.[304] The Master painted a magnificent panorama of the future that would be possible if the believers were united, joyous, grateful, and selfless:

> … Since the desire of all is unity and agreement, it is certain that this meeting will be productive of great results… This is a new Day, and this hour is a new Hour in which we have come together. Surely the Sun of Reality with its full effulgence will illumine us, and the darkness of disagreements will disappear… Such gatherings as this have no equal or likeness in the world of mankind, where people are drawn together by physical motives or in furtherance of material interests, for this meeting is a prototype of that inner and complete spiritual association in the eternal world of being.
>
> True Bahá'í meetings are the mirrors of the Kingdom wherein images of the Supreme Concourse are reflected. In them the lights of the most great guidance are visible… Hundreds of thousands of meetings shall be held to commemorate this occasion, and the very words I speak to you today shall be repeated in them for ages to come…
>
> Rejoice, for the heavenly table is prepared for you.
> Rejoice, for the angels of heaven are your assistants and helpers.
> Rejoice, for the glance of the Blessed Beauty, Bahá'u'lláh, is directed upon you.
> Rejoice, for Bahá'u'lláh is your Protector.
> Rejoice, for the everlasting glory is destined for you.
> Rejoice, for the eternal life is awaiting you.

> How many blessed souls have longed for this radiant century, their utmost hopes and desires centered upon the happiness and joy of one such day as this... God has favored you in this century and has specialized you for the realization of its blessings ...
>
> First, you must become united and agreed among yourselves... In the path of God one must forget himself entirely... It is my hope that you may become like this.³⁰⁵

The Master anointed each guest with attar of rose.³⁰⁶ When he finished, the sound of thunder could be heard and dark clouds were gathering. Juliet Thompson remembers 'Abdu'l-Bahá at that point walking a little way down the road with a few of the Persian men and seating himself in a chair which had been left there, then raising his face to the sky. A strong wind blew and parted the rain filled clouds, and the feast could continue.³⁰⁷ The guests ate Persian pilaf, sherbet and sweet.³⁰⁸

Many guests lingered late into the evening. 'Abdu'l-Bahá sat in a chair on the top step of the porch surrounded by Juliet Thompson, Lua Getsinger, May Maxwell, Marjorie Morten, Silvia Gannett, and a young man, Neval Thomas. Out in front of him sat many guests holding long thin candles which sparkled in the gathering dusk— "like great moths and the burning tips of the tapers they waved like fireflies darting about"³⁰⁹—seekers who by their nature could not pull themselves away from the presence of the Master.

'Abdu'l-Bahá spent the night is West Englewood. The following day, Sunday, June 30th, he was invited to the home of the Persian Consul General, Mr. Topakyan, in Morristown, NJ.³¹⁰

The irony of this invitation was that in Persia itself, Bahá'ís were being actively persecuted. The machinations of clerics, government leaders, and Covenant breakers had caused the banishment and imprisonment of Bahá'u'lláh and His family and decades of suffering for 'Abdu'l-Bahá. Persecutions of Bahá'ís were increasing again as a result of the breakdown of the authority of the Qajar dynasty that ruled Persia.

Mr. Topakyan had met 'Abdu'l-Bahá before at the May 13th meeting of the New York Peace Society. On that evening he had extolled 'Abdu'l-Bahá's position with respect to Persia, the land that had persecuted him:

> Our guest of honor has stood as a Prophet of enlightenment and peace for the Persian Empire, and a well-wisher of Persia may well

honor him… I am happy to say that Abdu'l-Baha is the Glory of Persia today.[311]

At this lunch, Mr. Topakyan showed great deference to 'Abdu'l-Bahá and had invited several prominent public people, reporters, and photographers.

During 'Abdu'l-Bahá's time in New York City, creative people and activists wanted to meet him. Louis Potter, a nationally known sculptor, was an active seeker in his spiritual life and came to visit in May. He had traveled for his art as far as Africa and Alaska where he sculpted the Tlingit Eskimos in 1905.[312] He also made a medallion with the image of 'Abdu'l-Bahá.[313] Potter was greatly moved by meeting the Master, but he chose to continue his spiritual search and went out to the West Coast where he met a 'Chinese mystic' and herbalist who gave him extract from a peach tree root which killed him.[314]

At a reception in the home of Mrs. Tatum in May, Sarah Graham Mulhall sought out the presence of 'Abdu'l-Bahá. Her father and brother had been deeply involved in researching the effects of drugs on the human body and had died, possibly as a result of their dangerous work. The Master strongly encouraged her to continue in this line of work. She went on to become the first Narcotics Commissioner for the City of New York, appointed by Gov. Al Smith. She personally led a drug raid on wealthy men, some of whom were great supporters of St. John's and St. Patrick's Cathedrals. The men were all brought to trial, though the Commissioner's office was eventually abolished under pressure from the Bishop.[315]

Khán Báhádúr Alláh-Bakhsh, the Governor of Lahore, Pakistan, had become interested in meeting 'Abdu'l-Bahá after learning of the Faith from Juliet Thompson. The elderly governor spent a long time with the Master and later wrote Juliet that 'Abdu'l-Bahá is the "Divine Light of today".[316] The Master had responded to this governor's spiritual interests. Otherwise, he might not have agreed to meet with politicians as they often just wanted to bolster their own image. For instance, he did not accept the Mayor of New York City's request that he be his guest in the reviewing stand for the City's Fourth of July parade, sending representatives instead.[317]

'Abdu'l-Bahá always gave of his time and energy when it was for the purpose of creating unity among the believers. For example, he participated in the July wedding of Harlan and Grace Ober. Harlan Ober had been asked in 1907, after having been a Bahá'í for only a few months, to go with Hooper Harris on a teaching trip to India and

Burma. India and Burma were, after Persia and the United States, the third area in the world with a significant concentration of Bahá'ís, and 'Abdu'l-Bahá was eager to have Western believers go there as a way of uniting East and West.[318]

The Master was not averse to using different means to publicize his visit as this would create greater awareness of the Faith. Soon after he arrived in New York City, a moving picture company asked permission to film him. Some Bahá'ís were against this as the Master's image would be shown in theaters, but he readily approved. In the footage, 'Abdu'l-Bahá approaches the camera while exhorting Bahá'u'lláh to bless this effort as a means of spreading the Faith.[319]

Hearst's Magazine wrote of 'Abdu'l-Bahá:

> One distinguishable and peculiar thing about Abdul-Baha is that he does not make war upon, or even criticize, any other religious faith… No man of recent times has shown such a magnificent affirmative spirit as this man Abdul-Baha… He listens with much appreciation and sympathy and when he speaks it is slowly, distinctly, and most impressively. He knows what he is saying. His heart is full and his emotions are brimming, although kept well under control… He is reverential, respectful, filled with great and holy zeal. And this zeal takes the form of a message of unification to the world.[320]

An editorial in the Independent, gave a more cynical description:

> Bahaism is not to be classed with the freak or fake religions which arise among us or are brought to us from abroad. Perhaps there are among its American disciples some of the class who take up with bahaism because bridge is going out…[321]

> His message, coming from the most turbulent and dissentious country of the globe, is an appeal for love, peace and unity. He shows how strife and enmity defeat the aims of humanity in every field… A strange offshoot from Mohammedanism in these latter days—this religion of universal peace, mutual toleration and equal rights. Tho its lessons may be most needed in Islam, yet they are far from being superfluous to Christendom.[322]

Harper's Weekly published an article with a broader view titled, "A Ray from the East":

> "Inasmuch," says Abdul-Baha Abbas, "as the reality of religions is one, and the difference is one of imitations, but religion essentially is one, the existing religions must give up the imitations in order that

the Reality may enlighten them all, may unite humanity… God has created all humanity; He has provided for all; He preserves all, and all are submerged in the ocean of his mercy… It must have become quite clear long ago to readers that we have here exactly the same thoughts, expressed in almost exactly the same words, as have made the material of religious urging and teaching for hundreds of years. Paul said, at Athens, before the sixtieth year of our era, exactly what Abbas Effendi repeats, in Chicago, at the beginning of the twentieth century."[323]

The July 1st edition of the New York Times announced that Woodrow Wilson had been nominated to be the candidate of his party. As President, Wilson would push for an international organization to help bring about and maintain international peace. Shoghi Effendi would write of Wilson:

> To [America's] President, the immortal Woodrow Wilson, must be ascribed the unique honor, among the statesmen of any nation, whether of the East or of the West, of having voiced sentiments so akin to the principles animating the Cause of Bahá'u'lláh, and of having more than any other world leader, contributed to the creation of the League of Nations—achievements which the pen of the Center of God's Covenant acclaimed as signaling the dawn of the Most Great Peace, …[324]

Chapter 9

Last Days: Farewell to America

'Abdu'l-Bahá Leaving the U.S.

AFTER HIS stay in New Jersey, 'Abdu'l-Bahá spent the first two weeks of July in New York City before embarking on a cross-country rail trip. He spoke most days to seekers at the Champney home at 309 West 78th St. which he had rented.

On July 1st, the Master spoke about wealth distribution, a topic which was on the minds of the many people who were attracted to the socialist and communist ideals of social leveling and the sharing of wealth. The 20th century would see social leveling in Russia and China resulting in extraordinary levels of state-sponsored famine, torture, and executions, with death estimates which are incomprehensible. The answer was the individual's adherence to spiritual reality:

> When a rich man believes and follows the Manifestation of God, it is a proof that his wealth is not an obstacle and does not prevent him from attaining the pathway of salvation. After he has been tested and tried, it will be seen whether his possessions are a hindrance in his religious life. But the poor are especially beloved of God. Their lives are full of difficulties, their trials continual, their hopes are in God alone. Therefore, you must assist the poor as much as possible, even by sacrifice of yourself.[325]

Distribution of wealth was a responsibility of governments and individuals:

> The greatest means for prevention is that whereby the laws of the community will be so framed and enacted that it will not be possible for a few to be millionaires and many destitute.[326]

Each person had a place and a role:

> Each in his station in the social fabric must be competent—each in his function according to ability but with justness of opportunity for all.[327]

Social leveling was completely contrary to the natural order of human life; justice was the operating principle at every level of human society.

In the next series of talks, 'Abdu'l-Bahá presented Bahá'u'lláh as the source of authority whose Word determined reality:

> Bahá'u'lláh says, "The universe hath neither beginning nor ending." He has set aside the elaborate theories and exhaustive opinions of scientists and material philosophers by the simple statement, "There is no beginning, no ending."[328]

> In this century when the beneficent results of unity and the ill effects of discord are so clearly apparent, the means for the attainment and accomplishment of human fellowship have appeared in the world.

Bahá'u'lláh has proclaimed and provided the way by which hostility and dissension may be removed from the human world. He has left no ground or possibility for strife and disagreement.[329]

The teachings specialized in Bahá'u'lláh are addressed to humanity. He says, "Ye are all the leaves of one tree." He does not say, "Ye are the leaves of two trees: one divine, the other satanic." He has declared that each individual member of the human family is a leaf or branch upon the Adamic tree; …[330]

Bahá'u'lláh declared that religion is in complete harmony with science and reason. If religious belief and doctrine is at variance with reason, it proceeds from the limited mind of man and not from God; therefore, it is unworthy of belief and not deserving of attention; … Reason is the first faculty of man, and the religion of God is in harmony with it. Bahá'u'lláh has removed this form of dissension and discord from among mankind and reconciled science with religion by revealing the pure teachings of the divine reality. This accomplishment is specialized to Him in this Day.[331]

Bahá'u'lláh said that God has sent religion for the purpose of establishing fellowship among humankind and not to create strife and discord, for all religion is founded upon the love of humanity.[332]

Other sources of human dissension are political, racial and patriotic prejudices. These have been removed by Bahá'u'lláh. He has said, and has guarded His statement by rational proofs from the Holy Books, that the world of humanity is one race, the surface of the earth one place of residence and that these imaginary racial barriers and political boundaries are without right or foundation.[333]

Diversity of languages has been a fruitful cause of discord… Sixty years ago Bahá'u'lláh advocated one language as the greatest means of unity and the basis of international conference. He wrote to the kings and rulers of the various nations, recommending that one language should be sanctioned and adopted by all governments. According to this each nation should acquire the universal language in addition to its native tongue.[334]

Lack of equality between man and woman is, likewise, a cause of human dissension. Bahá'u'lláh has named this as an important factor of discord and separation, for so long as humankind remains unequally divided in right and importance between male and female, no unity can be established.[335]

The day after the Master made most of these comments at the All Souls Unitarian Church at Fourth Ave. and Twentieth St., he spoke on thankfulness at the home of Dr. Florian Krug and Mrs. Grace Krug.

The Bahá'í women met weekly at the Krug home.³³⁶ The Krugs would be present in 'Akká the evening 'Abdu'l-Bahá passed away in November, 1921; Dr. Krug took photos of the funeral.³³⁷ Grace remembers the evening of the passing of the Master:

> We retired as usual, but Dr. Krug had a premonition that he would be called to the Master's bedside before morning. About one fifteen o'clock we were awakened by screams from the Master's house, "Come Dr. Krug, the Master, the Master!" Like a flash, the Doctor was up, dressed, out of the room and across the garden into the house. You see, friends, had we not occupied Abdu'l-Baha's room over the garage, Dr. Krug could not have reached the Master so quickly. I stood absolutely petrified with fear. Finally I was able to slip a one piece dress over my night robe and rushed after the Doctor. Friends, how can I describe that scene in the Master's bedroom! Dr. Krug stood in the center, his hand raised, saying: "Silence, our Beloved Master has ascended." I ran to His bedside and there He lay in the majesty of death. His lovely eyes were still open, but the light of love and understanding that had for so many years cheered the souls of men was gone! My, first thought was, my Adored One is freed from our endless questions, freed from His life of servitude and headaches. I turned and knelt at the feet of His sister, the Greatest Holy Leaf, put my head in her lap and in that agonized moment, she stroked my head and tried to comfort me. Friends, not one thought of herself! God has never created a more glorious woman than she!³³⁸

After the visit to the Krug home, 'Abdu'l-Bahá left New York City for four months on a trip that would take him to the West coast and back. During these months, war broke out in Europe, just as 'Abdu'l-Bahá had warned. The First Balkan War pitted the Bulgarians, Greeks, Albanians and Montenegrans, against the Ottoman Empire over control of the Ottoman's European provinces. It was this same part of the world which lit the fuse that became the conflagration of World War One in 1914. The war may have raised the prejudice among Americans towards Turks as 'Abdu'l-Bahá and the Persian believers were turned down at some hotels because the staff thought they were Turks.³³⁹

When 'Abdu'l-Bahá returned to New York City in mid-November after his cross-country teaching trip, he rented the Champney house at 309 West 78th St.. The house was near Riverside Park which ran for four miles along the Hudson River. This park was designed by Frederick Law Olmsted, a genius who had no college education but became the superintendent of Central Park in New York City and head of the organization that later became the American Red Cross. He was also passionate about preserving nature for the public good and worked on the preservation of Yosemite Valley and Niagara Falls. His firm worked on over five hundred projects, including college campuses and the grounds of the Capitol Building in Washington DC. The true impact of his life's work was only realized later. Near the end of his life, he had a complete mental breakdown and died in an asylum.

The beauty of Olmsted's Riverside Park was much appreciated by the Master. When he needed a break from the constant interaction with people, he liked to go to the Park and be refreshed by nature. Sometimes he lay down in the grass; other times he sat on a bench or walked.

On November 12th, 'Abdu'l-Bahá granted a private meeting to one of the most influential of all Americans: Andrew Carnegie. Born in Scotland, Carnegie grew up poor because his father, a weaver, was made redundant by new steam-powered looms which put many weavers out of work. The knowledge that his father had to beg for work deeply affected his son, and his mother decided to move the family to Pittsburg, PA, to try making a better life. Carnegie worked his way up the Pennsylvania Railroad and then moved into the iron and steel business where he showed his genius for seeing where things were going in the world. By 1900, his company was producing more steel than Great Britain. While he had the drive and talent for making money, Andrew was also deeply interested in the rights of workers, though the Homestead Strike in 1892 in which his workers were killed, damaged his image, and in international peace—he was one of the first prominent citizens to call for the League of Nations. He endowed the Peace Palace in The Hague, Netherlands, which today houses the World Court.[340] He sold his steel company for $480 million to J.P. Morgan, another titan of American industry, who, by his sixties, may well have been the richest man in the world.[341] He was determined to contribute his money to the betterment of society and went on to give away $350 million by building thousands of libraries—an employer's small library which he had used to educate himself had been available to him as a teenager—and endowing institutions of higher learning (Carnegie Mellon University), cultural institutions (Carnegie Hall, NYC), think tanks (Carnegie Endowment for Peace), research institutions (Carnegie Institute of Washington for scientific research), trusts to directly assist people (Carnegie Dunfermline Trust to assist the residents of Dunfermline Scotland where Carnegie was born), among many others.[342]

Carnegie's interest in the rights of workers, international peace and the betterment of society, may well have led him to seek an interview with the Master. After this private interview, the two corresponded and one of these letters was the basis of an article published in the New York Times in 1915, though it was written just a year and a half before World War One exploded:

> To the noble personage, his Excellency Mr. Andrew Carnegie: May God assist him!
>
> ... All the leaders and statesmen of Europe are thinking on the plane of war and the annihilation of the mansion of humanity, but thou (Carnegie) art thinking on the plane of peace and love and the strengthening and reinforcement of the basis of the superstructure of the human world. They are the heralds of death, thou art the harbinger of life. The foundations of their palaces are unstable and wavering and the turrets of their mansions are tottering and crumbling, but the basis of thy structure is firm and unmovable ...
>
> ...Today the most important object of the kingdom of God is the promulgation of the cause of universal peace and the principle of the oneness of the world of humanity. Whosoever arises in the accomplishment of this preeminent service the confirmations of the holy spirit will descend upon him ...
>
> ... Therefore, before long a vast and unlimited field will be opened before your view for the display of your powers and energies. You must promote this glorious intention with the heavenly power and the confirmation of the holy spirit. I am praying in thy behalf that thou mayest erect a pavilion and unfurl a flag in the world of peace, love, and eternal life ...[343]

'Abdu'l-Bahá also blessed J.P. Morgan, the leading American industrialist and a benefactor of schools, hospitals and museums, when he visited the Morgan Library, which housed Morgan's art and book collection, on E. 36th St.. He wrote a note in the guest book, translated as:

> O, Thou Generous Lord, verily this famous personage has done considerable philanthropy, render him great and dear in Thy Kingdom, make him happy and joyous in both worlds, and confirm him in serving the world of humanity, and submerge him in the sea of Thy Favors.[344]

'Abdu'l-Bahá made great efforts to unify believers in the United States by counseling and guiding them both in person and in writing with a spirit of loving affection, and hosting them in gatherings to promote unity.

Individuals often struggled to put into practice the spiritual teaching the Master gave them, especially when it came to unity. Juliette Thompson had been engaged to Mason Remey but then broke it off. They made every effort to avoid each other. Then she resolved to go to him and recommend that they visit 'Abdu'l-Bahá together and say that they were reconciled and would be brothers and sisters in the Cause. Before this happened, another believer told her that 'Abdu'l-Bahá wished for Juliet to marry Remey. Juliet went directly to the Master who told her the believer had misunderstood; according to Juliet he answered, "I never interfere. Mrs. Hopper came and told me that she wanted to unite you and Mr. Remey. I said 'Very well, try.' But it is just as I wrote you long ago. Unless there is perfect agreement—perfect harmony—love, these things are not good".[345] Juliet interpreted this statement just in terms of her and Remey, not any deeper than that for she resolved after this never to see Remey again.[346]

He always counseled individuals lovingly but, when it came to Covenant breaking, he took a more severe, corrective approach. Dr. Ibráhím Kheiralla had been the original teacher of the Faith in the United States, and many people had become interested in the Faith through him so when he returned from pilgrimage and broke the Covenant by turning against the Master, many became estranged from the Faith. 'Abdu'l-Bahá characterized Covenant-breaking as a spiritual poison. Bahá'ís must absolutely shun the Covenant-breaker to prevent the contagion from spreading. The Covenant was the pivot around which the Bahá'í community was united, so breaking the Covenant fragmented it and could, if allowed, cause conflict on a much larger scale impairing the very mission of the Faith.

When 'Abdu'l-Bahá came to the United States, he commissioned Howard MacNutt to go to Chicago where Kheiralla's Covenant-breaking had done the most damage and tell the believers in clear and certain terms that they must have no interaction with the Covenant- breakers and to warn them of the consequences of this poison. This may have been a difficult task for MacNutt whose spirituality was focused on the idea of "unity through love" and who had been appointed by Kheiralla as the teacher of New York City. When he returned, it was clear that MacNutt had not carried out the task fully. On November 15th,

'Abdu'l-Bahá showed MacNutt a letter recently written by MacNutt to a Dr. Nutt who continued his friendship with Kheiralla, and the Master had to warn him that continuing contact like this placed MacNutt in danger.[347] MacNutt had also written to Dr. Zia Baghdadi that he had found the wavering believers in Chicago to be "angels".[348]

MacNutt's lack of firmness must have saddened 'Abdu'l-Bahá; he had told Juliet Thompson that he measured the love of the believers by their degree of obedience. So in the evening of November 19th, MacNutt came to meet the Master again at the Kinney home and went into a private audience with him on the second floor. An eager crowd had gathered below to hear the Master. As the two emerged, Juliet Thompson heard 'Abdu'l-Bahá tell MacNutt to go downstairs and say to the crowd "I was like Saul. Now I am Paul, for I see", to which MacNutt astonishingly replied, "But I don't see". 'Abdu'l-Bahá then commanded him to follow through with this, and MacNutt went downstairs and spoke those words to the assemblage. As he spoke, somewhat hesitatingly, the Master was listening from upstairs and closed his eyes as if in prayer. When MacNutt came back upstairs the Master embraced him.[349]

But it seems that MacNutt continued to waver. In a cable to 'Alí-Kuli Khán April 16th, 1913, 'Abdu'l-Bahá wrote, "Macnutt repented from violation of covenant but was not awakened." It would take several more months of correspondence for 'Abdu'l-Bahá to be satisfied with MacNutt's convictions and recognize him as a Baha'i again. MacNutt would continue his life of service. When he retired to Miami, he actively taught the Faith to African-Americans, having finally overcome his feelings of racism.[350]

On the 18th, 'Abdu'l-Bahá had dinner with the poet Frank K. Moxey and his wife. The following year in July, while he was in Port Said, Egypt, he received a packet of Mr. Moxey's poems. He asked that the titles be read to him and then that the poem on the Báb be translated. The Master was moved by the poem and expressed the hope that Moxey would continue to write such poetry as America needed a Bahá'í poet while there were many in Persia.[351]

During these last two weeks in New York City, 'Abdu'l-Bahá continued to instruct the believers, but he turned down most offers to speak publicly. At the home of Juliet Thompson on November 15th, he gave an uncharacteristically long talk on the life of Bahá'u'lláh and enumerated some of the fundamental principles taught by Bahá'u'lláh. The following day, he explained the purpose of the Manifestation of God which must have radically changed the perceptions of his audience about religion because he asserted that the Manifestations of God had come to 'train' and 'educate' the souls of people not raise up new buildings:

> The purpose of the appearance of the Manifestations of God is the training of the people. That is the only result of Their mission, the real outcome. The outcome of the whole life of Jesus was the training of eleven disciples and two women. Why did He suffer troubles, ordeals and calamities? For the training of these few followers. That was the result of His life. The product of the life of Christ was not the churches but the illumined souls of those who believed in Him. Afterward, they spread His teachings.[352]

At the Moxey home on the 18th, he continued with this theme challenging people's standard conception of religion:

> The supreme and most important happening in the human world is the Manifestation of God and the descent of the law of God. The holy, divine Manifestations did not reveal themselves for the purpose of founding a nation, sect or faction. They did not appear in order that a certain number might acknowledge Their Prophethood. They did not declare Their heavenly mission and message in order to lay the foundation for a religious belief. Even Christ did not become manifest that we should merely believe in Him as the Christ, follow Him and adore His mention. All these are limited in scope and requirement, whereas the reality of Christ is an unlimited essence.[353]

At the home of the Kinneys, the Master exhorted believers to develop the Divine virtues, challenging them with the standard of a true Bahá'í:

> You must manifest complete love and affection toward all mankind. Do not exalt yourselves above others, but consider all as your equals, ... Never speak disparagingly of others, but praise without distinction... Recognize your enemies as friends, and consider those who wish you evil as the wishers of good... Act in such a way that your heart may be free from hatred... Do not complain of others. Refrain from reprimanding them, and if you wish to give admonition or advice, let it be offered in such a way that it will not burden the bearer... Beware! Beware! lest ye offend any heart... Be the source of consolation to every sad one, assist every weak one, be helpful to every indigent one, care for every sick one, be the cause of glorification to every lowly one, and shelter those who are overshadowed by fear.

In brief, let each one of you be as a lamp shining forth with the light of the virtues of the world of humanity. Be trustworthy, sincere, affectionate and replete with chastity. Be illumined, be spiritual, be divine, be glorious, be quickened of God, be a Bahá'í.[354]

When the believers tried to give him gifts, he told them that the greatest gift they could give him was their unity.

At the Kinney home on December 2nd, 'Abdu'l-Bahá again gave a talk in which he set forth the principles brought by Bahá'u'lláh as well as re-emphasizing the need for a Covenant and its unique place in the history of religion:

> As to the most great characteristic of the revelation of Bahá'u'lláh, a specific teaching not given by any of the Prophets of the past: It is the ordination and appointment of the Center of the Covenant… To ensure unity and agreement He has entered into a Covenant with all the people of the world, including the interpreter and explainer of His teachings, so that no one may interpret or explain the religion of God according to his own view or opinion and thus create a sect founded upon his individual understanding of the divine Words. The Book of the Covenant or Testament of Bahá'u'lláh is the means of preventing such a possibility, … There are some people of self-will and desire who do not communicate their intentions to you in clear language… Yet there are some who for the sake of personal interest and prestige will attempt to sow the seeds of sedition and disloyalty among you. To protect and safeguard the religion of God from this and all other attack, the Center of the Covenant has been named and appointed by Bahá'u'lláh.[355]

He gave only three talks in public forums during these last weeks. The first took place on November 17th, at the Genealogical Hall. The New York Genealogical and Biographical Society was founded in 1869, the purpose of which was "to discover, procure, preserve and perpetuate whatever may relate to Genealogy and Biography, and more particularly to the genealogies and biographies of families, persons and citizens associated and identified with the State of New York",[356] and it had grown rapidly such that by 1912 it was purchasing another building.[357] Possibly because of the name of the hall, the Master spoke there about the development of society and how the human race had reached its stage of maturity.

Another public talk was given at the Theosophical Society on December 4th. The Society had been founded in 1875 as a center for the application of teachings of an extraordinary woman, Helena Petrovan Blavatsky. She was born in Russia, married the governor of an Armenian province, traveled constantly to many parts of the world, became an accomplished musician, writer, self-proclaimed psychic and mystic, lived for awhile in Tibet and founded the Theosophical Society based on her spiritual ideas. She met an Indian guru in London and accepted him as her spiritual teacher and master because she had seen him in her childhood dreams.[358] The Theosophical Society taught that all existence was an interdependent whole, that this Reality which flowed through all things was transcendent, and that each human being had unique value. As a result, theosophists emphasized the equality and brotherhood of all people, the value of all religious traditions and the importance of altruism in human behavior. So, during his visit to the Theosophical Society, the Master touched on these subjects and spoke of the nature of reality and of Divinity, the common purpose of the Manifestations of God, and the spiritual reality of man.[359]

The most significant public appearance of 'Abdu'l-Bahá in those final weeks was the public celebration of the Day of the Covenant on November 23rd. A banquet was organized by the believers at the Great Northern Hotel at 118 W. 57th Street. This hotel would soon be one of the few in the City to welcome unaccompanied women travelers without making them adhere to strict rules. It advertised itself as "Quiet hotel; patronized by women traveling alone" where one could get a single room for $2.[360] But, in 1912, the hotel did not admit African-Americans. The Bahá'ís tried to convince the management to allow them to invite their African-American friends but the hotel vehemently refused citing business concerns that if they allowed African-Americans in, "no respectable person will ever set foot in it, and my business will go to the winds".[361]

Chandeliers dangled from the ceiling of the banquet hall over two long rectangular tables at which sat the guests. To the side, several other round tables were arranged behind large pillars for additional guests. The attire was formal. Flowers and crystal festooned the cloth covered tables. Light from electric bulbs sparkled in the glasses. At the front of the room the honored guests from Persia sat at a long table in front of flags of the United States and Persia, including Mr. Topakyan, the Persian consul general.[362]

When the Master walked in, all stood up and cried out, "Alláh'u'Abhá"!

> The effect of such an assembly as this is conducive to divine fellowship and strengthening of the bond which cements and unifies hearts. This is the indestructible bond of spirit which conjoins the East and West. By it the very foundations of race prejudice are uprooted and destroyed, the banner of spiritual democracy is hoisted

aloft, the world of religion is purified from superannuated beliefs and hereditary imitations of forms, and the oneness of the reality underlying all religions is revealed and disclosed… Every limiting and restricting movement or meeting of mere personal interest is human in nature. Every universal movement unlimited in scope and purpose is divine. The Cause of God is advanced whenever and wherever a universal meeting is established among mankind.[363]

He exhorted the attendees to:

…endeavor that your attitudes and intentions here tonight be universal and altruistic in nature. Consecrate and devote yourselves to the betterment and service of all the human race. Let no barrier of ill feeling or personal prejudice exist between these souls, for when your motives are universal and your intentions heavenly in character, when your aspirations are centered in the Kingdom, there is no doubt whatever that you will become the recipients of the bounty and good pleasure of God.[364]

After he had spoken, the Master walked around the room and blessed each guest with a drop of attar of rose—the extract from the petals of roses—from his own hands; Juliet Thompson felt her whole being "wake and sparkle"[365] when the drop of rose water touched her. The guests then sang a hymn in praise of the Master as he sat down.

To make up for the shameful exclusion of the African-American believers and friends from the hotel banquet, a feast was held for them at the Kinney home the next day. The white Bahá'í women served the food. Of this occasion, 'Abdu'l-Bahá said:

Today you have carried out the laws of the Blessed Beauty and have truly acted according to the teachings of the Supreme Pen. Behold what an influence and effect the words of Bahá'u'lláh have had upon the hearts, that hating and shunning have been forgotten and that prejudices have been obliterated to such an extent that you arose to serve one another with great sincerity.[366]

A *Tribune* article of the 24th, titled "ABDUL-BAHA GOING AWAY", announced the Master's departure:

Abdul-Baha, Abbas Effendi, the Persian Prophet and center of the Bahai movement, received assurances of unswerving loyalty last night from members of the Bahai assembly of New York City, who gathered at a farewell dinner in his honor at the Great Northern Hotel.[367]

The day of departure came. Several Bahá'ís accompanied him from the Emery home to the ship. Once there, more Bahá'ís arrived and walked up with him into a large cabin room. He stood up and spoke to them one last time, challenging them:

> This is my last meeting with you, for now I am on the ship ready to sail away. These are my final words of exhortation. I have repeatedly summoned you to the cause of the unity of the world of humanity, announcing that all mankind are the servants of the same God, that God is the creator of all; ... Your eyes have been illumined, your ears are attentive, your hearts knowing. You must be free from prejudice and fanaticism, beholding no differences between the races and religions. You must look to God, for He is the real Shepherd, and all humanity are His sheep... Consider how the Prophets Who have been sent, the great souls who have appeared and the sages who have arisen in the world have exhorted mankind to unity and love. This has been the essence of their mission and teaching... You must, therefore, look toward each other and then toward mankind with the utmost love and kindness. You have no excuse to bring before God if you fail to live according to His command, for you are informed of that which constitutes the good pleasure of God. You have heard His commandments and precepts... It is my hope that you may become successful in this high calling so that like brilliant lamps you may cast light upon the world of humanity and quicken and stir the body of existence like unto a spirit of life. This is eternal glory. This is everlasting felicity. This is immortal life. This is heavenly attainment. This is being created in the image and likeness of God. And unto this I call you, praying to God to strengthen and bless you.[368]

He sat back down in the corner of the large cabin room. Bahá'ís came up and crowded around him. Off to the side, Juliet Thompson wept quietly.

'Abdu'l-Bahá had gone across the American continent and back, spoken with people from the highest to the humblest positions in American society, exemplified in every aspect of his behavior the unity of the human race and, most of all, explained the Teachings of his Father.

The words he had spoken during these months would be memorialized in writing, and they would be a source of inspiration to people long after he had passed away.

The waves slapped the hull of the Celtic. The wind blew hats off some of the onlookers. The Master's light colored cloak and fez and long white beard contrasted with the grey background of the boat as he stood on the ship's deck. He looked out over the crowd below and raised his hand like a benediction.

He had done all he could do. Now, it was up to the believers whose feet remained on the ground.

"Bless Thou, O King of Kings, the city of New York! Cause the friends there to be kind to one another. Purify their souls and make their hearts to be free and detached. Illumine the world of their consciousness. Exhilarate their spirits and bestow celestial power and confirmation upon them. Establish there a heavenly realm, so that the City of Bahá may prosper and New York be favoured with blessings from the Abhá Kingdom, that this region may become like the all-highest Paradise, may develop into a vineyard of God and be transformed into a heavenly orchard and a spiritual rose garden."

'Abdu'l-Bahá, New York City, 1912

'Abdu'l-Bahá in Riverside Park

Endnotes

1. Allan L. Ward, *236 Days: Abdu'l-Bahá's Journey in America* (Wilmette, Il: Bahá'í Publishing Trust, 1979), 4-5.
2. Mahmúd Zarqani, Trans. by Mohi Sobhani with Shirley Marcias, *Mahmúd's Diary* (Oxford, UK: George Ronald, 1998), 28.
3. Ibid, 30.
4. 33.
5. Wendell Phillips Dodge, quoted in Ward, *236 Days: 'Abdu'l-Bahá's Journey in America*, 13.
6. Ibid, 14.
7. Zarqani, 35.
8. Ibid, 35-36.
9. 36.
10. 36.
11. Robert H. Stockman, *The Bahá'í Faith in America: Early expansion, 1900-1912* (Oxford, UK: George Ronald, 1995), 337-339.
12. Juliet Thompson, *Diary of Juliet Thompson*, accessed: September 20th, 2011 http://bahai-library.com/books/thompson/2.html, Chapter 3.
13. Ibid, Chapter 4.
14. Marzieh Gail, *"At 48 West 10th St"*, accessed: August 3rd, 2011 http://bahai-library.com/books/thompson/2.html.
15. Thompson, *Diary*, Chapter 4.
16. O.Z. Whitehead, *Some early Bahá'ís of the West* (Oxford, UK: George Ronald, 1976), 44-47.
17. Zarqani, 38.
18. Marzieh Gail, *Dawn over Mount Hira and other essays* (Oxford, UK: George Ronald, 1976), 203-204.
19. Ibid, 208.
20. Thompson, *Diary*, Chapter 4.
21. 'Abdu'l-Bahá, *Promulgation of Universal Peace* (Wilmette, IL: Bahá'í Publishing Trust, 1982), 3.
22. Zarqani, *Diary*, 38.
23. Howard Colby Ives, *Portals to Freedom* (Oxford, UK: George Ronald, 1990), 22-27.
24. Ibid, 29.
25. Zarqani, *Diary*, 38-39.
26. Ward, *236 days*, 17.
27. Ibid, 18.
28. 16.

29. 17.
30. Whitehead, *Some early Bahá'ís*, 35-36.
31. Robert Stockman, *"MacNutt, Howard"*, accessed: June 10th, 2011 http://bahai-library.com/stockman_macnutt.
32. Stockman, *The Bahá'í Faith in America: Early expansion, 1900-1912*, 233.
33. Ibid, 308.
34. Whitehead, *Some early Bahá'ís*, 36.
35. Stockman, *Early expansion*, 206-209.
36. Ibid.
37. 338.
38. Whitehead, *Some early Bahá'ís*, 38.
39. 'Abdu'l-Bahá, *Promulgation of Universal Peace*, 4-7.
40. Thompson, *Diary*, Chapter 4.
41. 'Abdu'l-Bahá, *Promulgation of Universal Peace*, 8-9.
42. Zarqani, *Diary*, 40.
43. Gertrude Buikema, Albert Windust, Mirza Ahmad Sohrab, editors, *Star of the West, Vol. III* Chicago (Aug 1, 1912) No. 8, 5
44. Ibid, 8.
45. 'Abdu'l-Bahá, *Promulgation of Universal Peace*, 9.
46. Zarqani, *Diary*, 41.
47. Thompson, *Diary*, Chapter 4.
48. Ibid, Chapter 4.
49. No author given, *"Parish history"*, accessed: August 13th, 2011, http://ascensionnyc.org/history
50. Thompson, *Diary*, Chapter 3.
51. Ibid, Chapter 4.
52. New International version, *"1 Corinthians 1"*, accessed: December 11th, 2011, http://www.biblegateway.com/passage/.
53. Thompson, Chapter 4.
54. 'Abdu'l-Bahá, *Promulgation of Universal Peace*, 11-12.
55. Ibid, 12.
56. 12.
57. 13.
58. Thompson, *Diary*, Chapter 4.
59. Zarqani, *Diary*, 43.
60. Thompson, *Diary*, Chapter 4.
61. Ibid, Chapter 4.
62. 'Abdu'l-Bahá, *Promulgation of Universal Peace*, 14.
63. Ibid, 14.

64. 15.
65. 15.
66. 15.
67. *Star of the West*, Vol. III, No. 7, 5, 10-11.
68. Thompson, *Diary*, Chapter 4.
69. National Spiritual Assembly of the Baha'is of the United States and Canada, *The Bahá'í World: A Biennial International Record, Vol. XI* (Wilmette, IL: Baha'i Publishing Committee, 1952), 509-510.
70. 'Abdu'l-Bahá, *Promulgation of Universal Peace*, 17.
71. Ibid, 17.
72. 17.
73. 17.
74. 18.
75. Thompson, *Diary*, Chapter 4.
76. 'Abdu'l-Bahá, *Promulgation of Universal Peace*, 19.
77. Ibid, 19.
78. 19.
79. Ward, *236 Days*, 23.
80. 'Abdu'l-Bahá, *Promulgation of Universal Peace*, 22.
81. Ibid, 23.
82. 24.
83. 24.
84. The sources differ on the events of April 18th and 19th, 1912:
    - Juliet Thompson records 'Abdu'l-Bahá's talk at the Bowery Mission and attendance at the play, "The Terrible Meek", as being on April 19th. She doesn't mention the Earl Hall talk.
    - Mahmúd Zarqani lists the Bowery Mission visit and the talk at the Emery home as being on the 18th. He doesn't mention "The Terrible Meek".
    - In the "Promulgation of Universal Peace", the talk at the Emery home is on the 18th and Earl Hall and the Bowery Mission are on the 19th.
    - Allen Ward has "The Terrible Meek" and the Bowery Mission on the 18th and Earl Hall on the 19th.
    - Kate Carew, the newspaper reporter, gives an account of her visit with 'Abdu'l-Bahá which has Earl Hall ("that day"), "The Terrible Meek" ("theater today") and the Bowery Mission on the same day.

    The key points in establishing the sequence of events are below:

- The two first-hand witnesses, Juliet Thompson and Kate Carew state that 'Abdu'l-Bahá went to see the "Terrible Meek" on the same day as the visit to the Bowery Mission.
- There is agreement in the sources which mention it that Earl Hall was on the 19th.
- The talks at the Emery home and the Bowery Mission must have been in the evenings because 'Abdu'l-Bahá begins them with "Tonight…". So they could only have been on the 18th and 19th respectively as there are no other nights available.

As a result of these conclusions, the authors have made the following reconstruction of 'Abdu'l-Bahá's schedule:
- Thursday, April 18th:
  Interviews at the Hotel Ansonia during the day
  Talk at the Emery home in the evening
- Friday, April 19
  Portrait by Khalil Gibran
  Earl Hall
  The Terrible Meek
  The Bowery Mission

85. Joyce Mendelsohn, *The Lower East Side remembered and revisited: a history and guide to a legendary New York neighborhood* (NY, NY: Columbia University Press September 11th, 2009).
86. 'Abdu'l-Bahá, *Promulgation of Universal Peace*, 28.
87. Juliet Thompson quoted in Whitehead, *Some early Bahá'ís*, 76.
88. Ibid, 76-77.
89. Guido Bruno, *"Fragments from Greenwich Village"*, accessed: July 19th, 2011 http://www.bohemianlit.com/full_text/bruno/fragments.htm.
90. No author given, *"Ephemeral New York"*, accessed: July 23rd, 2011 http://ephemeralnewyork.wordpress.com/tag/greenwich-village-in-the1910s/.
91. Marzieh Gail, *"Juliet remembers Gibran as told to Marzieh"*, *World Order: A Bahá'í Magazine*, v. 12, n. 4 (Summer 1978): 29-31, accessed: July 1st, 2011 http://bahai-library.com/histories/juliet.gibran.html.
92. Marzieh Gail, *"Juliet remembers Gibran as told to Marzieh"*, 29-31
93. Kahlil Gibran quoted in Suheil Bushrui and Joe Jenkins, *Kahlil Gibran: Man and Poet* (Oxford, UK: One World, 1998), 123-126.
94. Ibid.
95. 123-126.
96. 123-126.
97. 'Abdu'l-Bahá, *Promulgation of Universal Peace*, 30.

98. Ibid, 31.
99. 31.
100. 31.
101. Barbara Schmidt, *"Kate Carew, "The only woman caricaturist""*, April 9th, 1997, accessed: August 3rd, 2011 http://www.twainquotes.com/interviews/confessions.html.
102. Denis Brian, *Pulitzer: A Life* (NY, NY: John Wiley and Sons, 2001), 129.
103. Schmidt, *"Kate Carew"*.
104. Ibid.
105. Ibid.
106. Ibid.
107. Ibid.
108. Ward, *236 Days*, 27.
109. Ibid, 28.
110. 30.
111. 31.
112. 32.
113. 33.
114. 33.
115. No author given, *"Tenements"*, accessed: July 15th, 2011 http://www.history.com/topics/tenements.
116. Maggie Blanck, *"New York City, Tenement life"*, May, 2010, viewed: August 2nd, 2011 http://maggieblanck.com/NewYork/Life.html.
117. Zarqani, *Diary*, 41.
118. Blanck, *"Tenement Life"*.
119. No author given, *"Our history in brief"*, accessed: July 7th, 2011 http://www.bowery.org/about-us/history/#1890s.
120. Ward, *236 Days*, 33.
121. Thompson, *Diary*, Chapter 4. She does not list the names of the "Persian believers".
122. 'Abdu'l-Bahá, *Promulgation of Universal Peace*, 32.
123. Ibid.
124. 32-33.
125. 33.
126. 33.
127. 34.
128. 34.
129. Thompson, *Diary*, Chapter 4.
130. Ward, *236 Days*, 35.

131. Ibid, 34.
132. Thompson, *Diary*, Chapter 4.
133. Ibid.
134. Ibid.
135. Ibid.
136. Ibid. According to *"Mahmúd's Diary"* (Zarqani, 47) "…some money was left over; which was given to other destitute people and children outside the Bowery."
137. US Department of Justice, *"WW I casualties and death tables"*, accessed: July 30th, 2011 http://www.pbs.org/greatwar/resources/casdeath_pop.html.
138. Michael Clodfelter, *Warfare and Armed Conflicts-A Statistical Reference to Casualty and Other Figures, 1500–2000 2nd Ed.*, (Jefferson, NC: McFarland & Company, 2002)
139. Michael Duffy, *"Weapons of war – Poison gas"*, accessed August 10th, 2011 http://www.firstworldwar.com/weaponry/gas.htm.
140. Ibid.
141. Michael Duffy, *"Life in the Trenches"*, accessed August 10th, 2011 http://www.firstworldwar.com/features/trenchlife.htm.
142. Prof. Joanna Bourke, *"Shell Shock during World War One"*, accessed: August 11th, 2011 http://www.bbc.co.uk/history/worldwars/wwone/shellshock_01.shtml.
143. No author given, *"Wilfred Owen, The Sentry"*, 2006, accessed: July 20th, 2011 http://www.englishverse.com/poems/the_sentry.
144. Saxon books, *"Wilfred Owen"*, 1999, accessed: July 20th, 2011 http://www.warpoetry.co.uk/owena.htm.
145. 'Abdu'l-Bahá, *Promulgation of Universal Peace*, 119.
146. Ibid, 114.
147. 115.
148. 115-116.
149. Zarqani, *Diary*, 91.
150. Paolo Enrico Coletta, *Presidency of William Howard Taft* (Kansas: University of Kansas Press, 1973), chapter 9.
151. 'Abdu'l-Bahá, *Promulgation of Universal Peace*, 117-118.
152. Ibid, 118.
153. 120.
154. 125.
155. 125.
156. Star of the West, Vol. III, No. 8, 11.
157. Ibid, 11.

158. 12-13.
159. 13.
160. 13.
161. No author given, *"New York Peace Records, 1815-1940"*, accessed: August 13th, 2011 http://www.gale.cengage.com/servlet/ItemDetailServlet?region=9&imprint=000&titleCode=SR632&type=4&id=D3575.
162. *Advocate for Peace, Vol. LXXII, #5* Boston May, 1910, American Peace Society, publisher.
163. Zarqani, 100.
164. Ahmad Sohrab to Agnes Parsons, May 15, 1912, Agnes Parsons Papers, quoted in Robert Stockman, *'Abdu'l-Bahá in America* (Wilmette, IL: Bahá'í Publishing Trust, 2012)
165. Sheperd, *"Mohonk Mountain House"*.
166. Janet Ruhe-Schoen, *"Who Will Bell the Cat?", 'Abdu'l-Bahá at Lake Mohonk"*, (not yet published).
167. Ibid.
168. No author given, *"What do Quakers believe?"*, accessed: July7th, 2011 http://www.quakerinfo.org/quakerism/beliefs.
169. Sok Hon Ham, *"Friends", New Encyclopedia Britannica, vol. 26, 15th ed.*, (Chicago IL: Encyclopaedia Britannica publisher, 1985), 255.
170. Sok Hon Ham, *Malssum/Quaker Sampaeknyon [The Messages & Friends for 300 Years; The History of Quakers]*, (Seoul, Korea: Hankilsa, 1988), 275. http://www2.gol.com/users/quakers/T&QNotes.htm.
171. Ibid.
172. International Peace Society, *"International Peace Society Records, 1917-1948"*, accessed: August 28th, 2011 http://www.swarthmore.edu/library/peace/CDGB/intpeacesociety.htm.
173. Ruhe-Schoen, *"Bell the Cat"*.
174. Sheperd, *"Mohonk Mountain House"*.
175. Letter of Charles Mason Remey to Albert K Smiley, April 25th, 1911, *Records of the Lake Mohonk Conference on International Arbitration, 1895-1937* (bulk 1895-1918), Collection: DG 054, Swarthmore College Peace Collection, Swarthmore, PA.
176. Ibid.
177. Mírzá 'Alí Kuli Khán, *"The conditions of universal peace"*, May 24th, 1911, Swarthmore College Peace Collection.
178. Ibid.
179. Ibid.
180. *"Persian American Educational Society"*, Swarthmore College Peace Collection.

181. Ahmad Sohrab to Mr. Phillips, letter dated September 1st, 2011, Swarthmore College Peace Collection.
182. 'Abdu'l-Bahá Abbás to Mr. Phillips, secretary of the Lake Mohonk Peace Conference, translated by Ahmad Sohrab, August 22nd, 1911. In a letter dated September 28th, 1911, from Mr. Phillips to Mr. Smiley, Mr. Phillips notes that, "Abdul Baha Abbas is evidently a person of considerable not and Mr. Sohrab obviously considers the document one of great value." Swarthmore College Peace Collection.
183. 'Alí Kuli Khán to Mr. H. C Phillips, letter dated October 17th, 1911, Swarthmore College Peace Collection.
184. Ibid.
185. Persian American Educational Society, *"An advanced statement concerning Abdul Baha's approaching visit to the United States"*, Swarthmore College Peace Collection.
186. 'Abdu'l-Bahá telegram to Mr. H. C. Phillips, May 4th, Swarthmore College Peace Collection.
187. Mírzá 'Alí Kuli Khán to Mr. H. C. Phillips, May 13th, 1911.
188. Anderson, Judith Icke, *William Howard Taft, an intimate portrait* (NY, NY: WW Norton and Co, 1981), 276.
189. *"General Program"*, Lake Mohonk Conference on International Arbitration, Eighteenth Annual Conference May 15-17, 1912, Swarthmore College Peace Collection.
190. Stockman, *Early expansion*.
191. *"Second Session"*, Report of the Eighteenth Annual Lake Mohonk Conference on International Arbitration, May 15th, 16th, and 17th, 1912, 42, Swarthmore College Peace Collection.
192. Ibid, 43.
193. 42-44.
194. Telegram from Ahmad Sohrab to Agnes Parsons, quoted in Stockman, *Early expansion*.
195. Ibid.
196. Zarqani, *Diary*, 102.
197. Rev. Frederick Lynch, at the Metropolitan Temple in New York *"Address at Metropolitan Temple Reception,"* Star of the West, vol. 3, no. 7 (July 13, 1912), 15, quoted in Stockman, *Early expansion*.
198. To Zia Baghdadi, quoted in Ruhe-Schoen, *"Bell the Cat"*.
199. In the wars of the twentieth century about 120 million people were slaughtered. At the beginning of the century 90 percent of those war casualties were soldiers. As the century ended over 90 percent of war casualties were civilians. Modern war is a direct assault on the

innocents . . ." Norman Etherington quoted in Douglas Mattern, *"Humanity's Juncture"*, The Humanist, 60:9, 2000, quoted in *"Making Peace"*, edited by Barry Hindess and Margaret Jolly, 2001, accessed: October 10th, 2011 http://www.imaginarymuseum.org/MHV/PZImhv/HindessThinkingPeace.html.
200. 'Abdu'l-Bahá, *Promulgation of Universal Peace*, 127.
201. Ibid, 150.
202. 158-9.
203. 172-3.
204. 154-5.
205. 147-8.
206. 148.
207. 148.
208. 149.
209. 152.
210. 161.
211. 151.
212. 168.
213. 163.
214. 165.
215. 175.
216. 126.
217. 201.
218. 153.
219. 166.
220. 163.
221. 157.
222. 158.
223. 164.
224. 204.
225. 171.
226. 171.
227. 171.
228. 157.
229. 167.
230. 167.
231. Stockman, *Early expansion*, 18.
232. 'Abdu'l-Bahá, *Promulgation of Universal Peace*, 167.
233. Ibid, 170.
234. 170-171.

235. 187.
236. 'Abdu'l-Bahá quoted in Stockman, *Early expansion*, 17.
237. Ibid.
238. 36.
239. 128.
240. 129.
241. 248.
242. 129.
243. 107.
244. 129.
245. 129.
246. 286.
247. 287.
248. Thompson, *Diary*, Chapter 4.
249. 'Abdu'l-Bahá, *Promulgation of Universal Peace*, 183.
250. Stockman, *Early expansion*, 126-7.
251. Ibid, 32.
252. Howard MacNutt, *"Unity through Love, 9"*, quoted in Stockman, *Early expansion*, 241.
253. Ibid, 240-241.
254. 242.
255. 307.
256. 242.
257. Whitehead, *Early Bahá'ís*, 131-135.
258. Isabella Brittingham, *"The Revelation of Bahá-ulláh"*, quoted in Whitehead, *Early Bahá'ís*, 132.
259. Edward Getsinger to the North Hudson Board of Council in May 1903, quoted in Stockman, *Early expansion*, 407.
260. Robert H. Stockman, *"Dodge, Arthur Pillsbury"*, *Bahá'í Encyclopedia Project*, accessed: December 11th, 2011 http://www.bahai-encyclopedia-project.org.
261. 'Abdu'l-Bahá in a letter to Ahmad Sohrab in Washington DC, June 16th, 1907, quoted in Stockman, *Early expansion*, 209-210.
262. Stockman, *"Dodge, Arthur Pillsbury"*.
263. Stockman, *Early expansion*, 21-22.
264. Ibid, 31-33.
265. 79.
266. 36-37.
267. 87-91.
268. 80-86.

269. 208.
270. *Star of the West* v. III, # 7, July 13, 1912, 9.
271. Ibid, 16-17.
272. *Star of the West* v. III, # 14 Nov. 23, 1912, 5.
273. *Star of the West* v. III #11, September 27th, 1912, 2.
274. *Star of the West* v. III #14, November 23rd, 1912, 10.
275. Ibid, 7.
276. Thompson, *Diary*, Chapter 4.
277. Ibid.
278. Ibid.
279. Ibid.
280. Ibid.
281. Zarqani, *Diary*, 137. Zarqani has this happening on the wrong day, Tuesday, June 18th, 1912.
282. Shoghi Effendi, *God Passes By* (Wilmette, IL: Bahá'í Publishing Trust, 1979), 288. The talk which 'Abdu'l-Bahá gave later that day of the sitting with Juliet Thompson described in this section is not recorded in any of the sources. Shoghi Effendi tells us that 'Abdu'l-Bahá named New York City, the City of the Covenant.
283. Shoghi Effendi, *"The Dispensation of Bahá'u'lláh", The World Order of Bahá'u'lláh* (Wilmette, IL: Bahá'í Publishing Trust, 1979), 132.
284. Ibid, 134.
285. Thompson, *Diary*, Chapter 4.
286. Zarqani, *Diary*, 141-142.
287. Ibid, 155.
288. 157.
289. 154.
290. Thompson, *Diary*, Chapter 4.
291. Ibid, Chapter 4.
292. Velda Piff Metalmann, *Lua Getsinger, Herald of the Covenant* (Oxford, UK: George Ronald, 1997), 151.
293. Ibid.
294. Thompson, *Diary*, Chapter 4.
295. Zarqani, *Diary*, 159.
296. Thompson, *Diary*, 272-273.
297. Zarqani, 65.
298. Ibid, 142.
299. 'Abdu'l-Bahá, *Promulgation of Universal Peace*, 206-207.

300. No author given, *"Decades of Pride Shattered"*, The New York Times, accessed: September 30, 2009 http://www.nytimes.com/1990/04/12/nyregion/decades-of-pride-shattered.html.
301. Roy Wilhelm quoted in *Bahá'í World*, vol. IX, 807, quoted in Whitehead, *Early Bahá'ís*, 89 -80.
302. Whitehead, *Early Bahá'ís*, 98.
303. Ibid, 99.
304. Zarqani, *Diary*, 148-149.
305. 'Abdu'l-Bahá, *Promulgation of Universal Peace*, 213-215.
306. Zarqani, *Diary*,150.
307. Thompson, *Diary*, Chapter 4.
308. Zarqani, *Diary*, 151.
309. Thompson, *Diary*, Chapter 4.
310. Zarqani, *Diary*, 152-3.
311. *Star of the West*, vol. III, #8, August 1, 1912, 13
312. No author given, *"Biography of Louis Potter"*, accessed September 18th, 2011 http://www.askart.com/AskART/artists/biography.aspx?searchtype=BIO&artist=26516.
313. Samuel Pennington, *"One American Art Medal Series"*, accessed September 15th, 2011 http://www.maineantiquedigest.com/medals/medalscolumn2.htm.
314. No author given, *"Peach poison killed Potter"*, The New York Times, September 1st, 1912 http://query.nytimes.com/mem/archivefree/pdf?res=F70B1EF83D5417738DDDA80894D1405B828DF1D3.
315. Thompson, *Diary*, Chapter 4.
316. Ibid.
317. Zarqani, *Diary*, 156.
318. Stockman, *Early expansion*, 266-271.
319. *Star of the West* vol. III, 9/8, #10.
320. Hubbard, "A Modern Prophet", *Hearst's Magazine*, July, 1912, quoted in Ward, *236 Days*, 105-107.
321. Ibid, 111.
322. 112-113.
323. 115-116.
324. Shoghi Effendi, *Citadel of Faith* (Wilmette, IL: Bahá'í Publishing Trust, 1980), 36.
325. 'Abdu'l-Bahá, *Promulgation of Universal Peace*, 216.
326. Ibid.
327. 216.
328. 220.

329. 230.
330. 230.
331. 231.
332. 231-2.
333. 232.
334. 232.
335. 233.
336. Zarqani, *Diary*, 387.
337. Editor, National Spiritual Assembly of the Bahá'ís of the United States, *"Dr. Florian Krug"*, accessed: September 20th, 2011 http://centenary.bahai.us/photo/dr-florian-krug-d-1924.
338. Grace Krug, *"Accounts of the Passing of 'Abdu'l-Baha"*, quoted in *World Order* vol. 7, No. 2, by Florian & Grace Krug, 38-41, quoted in *"Dr. Florian Krug d. 19124"*, accessed: October 2nd, 1912 http://centenary.bahai.us/photo/dr-florian-krug-d-1924.
339. Zarqani, *Diary*, 387.
340. No author given, *"Andrew Carnegie"*, accessed: October 3rd, 2011 http://www.vredespaleis.nl/.
341. No author given, *"Andrew Carnegie"*, accessed: October 4th, 2011 http://www.pbs.org/wgbh/amex/carnegie/peopleevents/pande01.html.
342. No author given, *"Andrew Carnegie's legacy"*, accessed: October 4th, 2011 http://carnegie.org/about-us/foundation-history/about-andrew-carnegie/carnegie-for-kids/andrew-carnegie-legacy/.
343. *Star of the West,* vol. VI, no 11, September 27 1915, and, No author given, *"Carnegie exalted by Bahaist leader"*, The New York Times, September 5th, 1915 http://query.nytimes.com/mem/archive-free/pdf?res=9E06E5DC1731E733A05756C0A96F9C946496D6CF.
344. Ward, 236 *Days,* 186-7.
345. Thompson, *Diary,* Chapter 4.
346. Ibid.
347. Stockman, *"MacNutt, Howard"*.
348. Thompson, *Diary,* Chapter 4.
349. Ibid.
350. Stockman, *"MacNutt, Howard"*.
351. 'Abdu'l-Bahá and Mírzá Ahmad Sohrab, *"Abdul-Baha in Egypt"*, accessed: October 5th 2011, http://bahai-library.com/sohrab_abdulbaha_egypt#51.
352. 'Abdu'l-Bahá, *Promulgation of Universal Peace*, 437.
353. Ibid, 442-443.

354. 453.
355. 455-6.
356. No author given, *"History of the NYG and B"*, accessed: October 5th, 2011 http://www.newyorkfamilyhistory.org/history-nygbs.
357. Ibid.
358. Adapted from Boris de Zirkoff, *"Biographical article on H. P. Blavatsky"*, Theosophia, (LA, CA), Summer 1968, 3-8, accessed: October 5th, 2011 http://www.blavatskyarchives.com/longseal.htm.
359. No author given, *"The Emily Sellon Memorial Library"*, accessed: October 5th, 2011 http://www.theosophy-ny.org/836.html.
360. Fremont Rider, *New York and vicinity, including Newark, Yonkers, and Jersey City* (NY, NY: Henry Holt and Company, 1916), 12, accessed: October 5th, 2011 http://www.archive.org/stream/ridersnewyorkcit00riderich/ridersnewyorkcit00riderich_djvu.txt
361. Zarqani, *Diary*, 407.
362. Ibid, 405.
363. 'Abdu'l-Bahá, *Promulgation of Universal Peace*, 447-448.
364. Ibid, 448.
365. Thompson, *Diary*, Chapter 4.
366. Zarqani, *Diary*, 407.
367. Ward, *236 Days*, 188.
368. Ibid, 468-470.

Bibliography

Books:

'Abdu'l-Bahá, *Promulgation of Universal Peace*, (Wilmette, IL: Bahá'í Publishing Trust, 1982)

Judith Icke Anderson, *William Howard Taft, an intimate portrait*, (NY, NY: WW Norton and Co, 1981)

Ronald H. Bayor, and Timothy J. Meagher, ed., *The New York Irish*, (Baltimore and London: Johns Hopkins University Press, 1991)

Denis Brian, *Pulitzer: A Life*, (NY, NY: John Wiley and Sons, 2001)

Gertrude Buikema, Albert Windust, Mirza Ahmad Sohrab, editors, *Star of the West, Vol. III-V, VII*, (Chicago, IL: Baha'i News Service, 1912-1913)

Suheil Bushrui and Joe Jenkins, *Kahlil Gibran: Man and Poet*, (Oxford, UK: One World, 1998)

Michael Clodfelter, *Warfare and Armed Conflicts-A Statistical Reference to Casualty and Other Figures, 1500–2000* 2nd Ed., (Jefferson, NC: McFarland & Company, 2002)

Shoghi Effendi, *Citadel of Faith*, (Wilmette, IL: Bahá'í Publishing Trust, 1980)

Shoghi Effendi, *God Passes By*, (Wilmette, IL: Bahá'í Publishing Trust, 1979)

Shoghi Effendi, *"The Dispensation of Bahá'u'lláh", The World Order of Bahá'u'lláh*, (Wilmette, IL: Bahá'í Publishing Trust, 1979)

Marzieh Gail, *Dawn over Mount Hira and other essays*, (Oxford, UK: George Ronald, 1976)

Sok Hon Ham, *"Friends"*, New Encyclopedia Britannica, vol. 26, 15th ed., (Chicago, IL: Encyclopaedia Britannica publisher, 1985) 255

Howard Colby Ives, *Portals to Freedom*, (Oxford, UK: George Ronald, 1990)

Paolo Enrico Coletta, *Presidency of William Howard Taft*, (Kansas: University of Kansas Press, 1973) Chapter 9

Joyce Mendelsohn, *The Lower East Side remembered and revisited: a history and guide to a legendary New York neighborhood*, (NY, NY: Columbia University Press, 2009)

Velda Piff Metalmann, Lua Getsinger, *Herald of the Covenant*, (Oxford, UK: George Ronald, 1997)

National Spiritual Assembly of the Baha'is of the United States and Canada, *The Bahá'í World: A Biennial International Record, Vol. XI*, (Wilmette, IL: Bahá'í Publishing Committee, 1952)

Janet Ruhe-Schoen, *"Who Will Bell the Cat?", 'Abdu'l-Bahá at Lake Mohonk"*, (not yet published)

Robert Stockman, *'Abdu'l-Bahá in America* (Wilmette, IL: Bahá'í Publishing Trust, 2012)

Robert H. Stockman, *The Bahá'í Faith in America: Early expansion, 1900-1912*, (Oxford, UK: George Ronald, 1995)

Swarthmore College Peace Collection, Swarthmore College, Swarthmore, PA:
- 'Abdu'l-Bahá Abbás to Mr. Phillips, secretary of the Lake Mohonk Peace Conference, translated by Ahmad Sohrab, August 22nd, 1911. In a letter dated September 28th, 1911, from Mr. Phillips to Mr. Smiley, Mr. Phillips notes that, "Abdul Baha Abbas is evidently a person of considerable not and Mr. Sohrab obviously considers the document one of great value."
- 'Abdu'l-Bahá telegram to Mr. H. C. Phillips, May 4th.
- 'Alí Kuli Khán to Mr. H. C Phillips, letter dated October 17th, 1911.
- Mírzá 'Alí Kuli Khán, *"The conditions of universal peace"*, May 24th, 1911.
- *"General Program"*, Lake Mohonk Conference on International Arbitration, Eighteenth Annual Conference May 15-17, 1912.
- *Records of the Lake Mohonk Conference on International Arbitration, 1895-1937* (bulk 1895-1918) Collection: DG 054, Swarthmore College Peace Collection, Swarthmore, PA
- *"Second Session"*, Report of the Eighteenth Annual Lake Mohonk Conference on International Arbitration, May 15th, 16th, and 17th, 1912, 42.
- Letter of Charles Mason Remey to Albert K Smiley, April 25th, 1911, *Records of the Lake Mohonk Conference on International Arbitration, 1895-1937* (bulk 1895-1918), Collection: DG 054.
- Ahmad Sohrab to Mr. Phillips, letter dated September 1st, 2011.
- Persian American Educational Society, *"An advanced statement concerning Abdul Baha's approaching visit to the United States"*.

Allan L. Ward, *236 Days: 'Abdu'l-Bahá's Journey in America*, (Wilmette, Il: Bahá'í Publishing Trust, 1979)

O.Z. Whitehead, *Some early Bahá'ís of the West*, (Oxford, UK: George Ronald, 1976)

Mahmúd Zarqani, *Mahmúd's Diary*, Trans. by Mohi Sobhani with Shirley Marcias, (Oxford, UK: George Ronald, 1998)

Web sites:

'Abdu'l-Bahá and Mírzá Ahmad Sohrab, *"Abdul-Baha in Egypt"*, (NY, NY: J.H. Sears and Company Inc., 1929) 51 http://bahai-library.com/sohrab_abdulbaha_egypt#51

Maggie Blanck, *"New York City, Tenement life"*, May, 2010, viewed: August 2nd, 2011 http://maggieblanck.com/NewYork/Life.html

Prof. Joanna Bourke, *"Shell Shock during World War One"*, last updated March 10th, 2011, viewed: August 11th, 2011 http://www.bbc.co.uk/history/worldwars/wwone/shellshock_01.shtml

Guido Bruno, *"Fragments from Greenwich Village"*, December 19th, 2010, viewed: July 19th, 2011 http://www.bohemianlit.com/full_text/bruno/fragments.htm

Michael Duffy, *"Weapons of war – Poison gas"*, August 22, 2009, viewed August 10th, 2011 http://www.firstworldwar.com/weaponry/gas.htm

Michael Duffy, *"Life in the Trenches"*, August 22, 2009, viewed August 10th, 2011 http://www.firstworldwar.com/features/trenchlife.htm

Editor, National Spiritual Assembly of the Bahá'ís of the United States, *"Dr. Florian Krug"*, viewed: September 20th, 2011 http://centenary.bahai.us/photo/dr-florian-krug-d-1924

Marzieh Gail, *"At 48 West 10th St"*, viewed: August 3rd, 2011 http://bahai-library.com/books/thompson/2.html

Marzieh Gail, *"Juliet remembers Gibran as told to Marzieh"*, WORLD ORDER: A Bahá'í Magazine, vol. 12, Number 4 (Summer 1978) 29-31, July 1st, 2011, viewed: July 1st, 2011 http://bahai-library.com/histories/juliet.gibran.html

Sok Hon Ham, *Malssum/Quaker Sampaeknyon [The Messages & Friends for 300 Years; The History of Quakers]*, (Seoul, Korea: Hankilsa, 1988) http://www2.gol.com/users/quakers/T&QNotes.htm

Grace Krug, *"Accounts of the Passing of 'Abdu'l-Baha"*, quoted in World Order Vol. 7, No. 2, by Florian & Grace Krug, 38-41, quoted in "Dr. Florian Krug d. 19124", viewed: October 2nd, 1912 http://centenary.bahai.us/photo/dr-florian-krug-d-1924

International Peace Society, *"International Peace Society Records, 1917-1948"*, viewed: August 28th, 2011 http://www.swarthmore.edu/library/peace/CDGB/intpeacesociety.htm

Sung Soo Kim, *"Historical and philosophical aspects of Quakerism"*, viewed: August 20th, 2011 http://www2.gol.com/users/quakers/T&QQuaker.htm

Douglas Mattern, *"Humanity's Juncture"*, The Humanist, 60:9, 2000, quoted in "Making Peace", edited by Barry Hindess and Margaret

Jolly, 2001 http://www.imaginarymuseum.org/MHV/PZImhv/HindessThinkingPeace.html

Wilfred Owen, *"Dulce et Decorum Est"*, August, 1977, viewed: August 10th, 2011 http://www.fordham.edu/halsall/mod/1914warpoets.html#owen1

Samuel Pennington, *"One American Art Medal Series"*, viewed September 15th, 2011 http://www.maineantiquedigest.com/medals/medalscolumn2.htm

Fremont Rider, *New York and vicinity, including Newark, Yonkers, and Jersey City,* (NY, NY: Henry Holt and Company 1916) http://www.archive.org/stream/ridersnewyorkcit00riderich/ridersnewyorkcit00riderich_djvu.txt

Saxon books, *"Wilfred Owen"*, 1999, viewed: July20th, 2011 http://www.warpoetry.co.uk/owena.htm

Barbara Schmidt, *"Kate Carew, "The only woman caricaturist""*, April 9th, 1997, viewed: August 3rd, 2011 http://www.twainquotes.com/interviews/confessions.html

Roger Sheperd, *"Mohonk Mountain House"*, August 21st, 2011, viewed: August 21st, 2011 http://rogershepherd.com/WIW/solution8/mohonk2.html

Robert Stockman, *"MacNutt, Howard"*, viewed: June 10th, 2011 http://bahai-library.com/stockman_macnutt

Robert H. Stockman, *"Thornton Chase"*, *Bahá'í Encyclopedia Project*, viewed: September 10th, 2011 http://www.bahai-encyclopedia-project.org

Juliet Thompson, *Diary of Juliet Thompson*, June 2002, viewed: September 20th, 2011 http://bahai-library.com/books/thompson/2.html

US Department of Justice, *"WW I casualties and death tables"*, viewed: July 30th, 2011 http://www.pbs.org/greatwar/resources/casdeath_pop.html

Adapted from Boris de Zirkoff, *"Biographical article on H. P. Blavatsky"*, *Theosophia*, (LA, CA), Summer 1968, 3-8 http://www.blavatskyarchives.com/longseal.htm

No author given, *"Andrew Carnegie"*, viewed: October 4th, 2011 http://www.pbs.org/wgbh/amex/carnegie/peopleevents/pande01.html

No author given, *"Andrew Carnegie"*, viewed: October 3rd, 2011 http://www.vredespaleis.nl/

No author given, *"Andrew Carnegie's legacy"*, viewed: October 4th, 2001http://carnegie.org/about-us/foundation-history/about-andrew-carnegie/carnegie-for-kids/andrew-carnegie-legacy/

No author given, *"Biography of Louis Potter"*, viewed September 18th, 2011 http://www.askart.com/AskART/artists/biography.aspx?searchtype=BIO&artist=26516

No author given, *"Carnegie exalted by Bahaist leader"*, The New York Times, September 5th, 1915 http://query.nytimes.com/mem/archive-free/pdf?res=9E06E5DC1731E733A05756C0A96F9C946496D6CF

No author given, *"Decades of Pride Shattered"*, The New York Times, April 12, 1990, viewed: September 30, 2009 http://www.nytimes.com/1990/04/12/nyregion/decades-f-pride-shattered.html

No author given, *"The Emily Sellon Memorial Library"*, viewed: October 5th, 2011 http://www.theosophy-ny.org/836.html

No author given, *"Ephemeral New York"*, January, 2008, viewed: July 23rd, 2011 http://ephemeralnewyork.wordpress.com/tag/greenwich-village-in-the1910s/

No author given, *"History of the NYG and B"*, viewed: October 5th, 2011 http://www.newyorkfamilyhistory.org/history-nygbs

No author given, *"New York Peace Records, 1815-1940"*, viewed: August 13th, 2011 http://www.gale.cengage.com/servlet/ItemDetailServlet?region=9&imprint=000&titleCode=SR632&type=4&id=D3575

No author given, *"Parish history"*, August 13th, 2011, viewed: August 13th, 2011 http://ascensionnyc.org/history/

No author given, *"Peach poison killed Potter"*, New York Times, September 1st, 1912 http://query.nytimes.com/mem/archive- free/pdf?res=F70B1EF83D5417738DDDA80894D1405B828DF1D3

No author given, *"Tenements"*, July 15th, 2011, viewed: July 15th, 2011 http://www.history.com/topics/tenements

No author given, *"What do Quakers believe?"*, July 7th, 2011, viewed: July 7th, 2011 http://www.quakerinfo.org/quakerism/beliefs

No author given, *"Wilfred Owen, The Sentry"*, 2006, viewed: July 20th, 2011 http://www.englishverse.com/poems/the_sentry

No author given, *"Our history in brief"*, viewed: July 7th, 2011 http://www.bowery.org/about-us/history/#1890s

Sok Hon Ham, *"Friends"*, New Encyclopedia Britannica, vol. 26, 15th ed., (Chicago IL: Encyclopaedia Britannica publisher 1985) 255

www.ingramcontent.com/pod-product-compliance
Lightning Source LLC
Chambersburg PA
CBHW022115040426
42450CB00006B/712